Building Street Rods

Ken Wickham

©2005 Ken Wickham
Published by

kp books
An Imprint of F+W Publications

**700 East State Street • Iola, WI 54990-0001
715-445-2214 • 888-457-2873**

Our toll-free number to place an order or obtain
a free catalog is (800) 258-0929.

All rights reserved. No portion of this publication may be reproduced or transmitted
in any form or by any means, electronic or mechanical, including photocopy, record-
ing, or any information storage and retrieval system, without permission in writing
from the publisher, except by a reviewer who may quote brief passages in a critical
article or review to be printed in a magazine or newspaper, or electronically transmitted on radio, television, or the Internet.

Library of Congress Catalog Number: 2005906836

ISBN: 0-87349-962-X

Designed by Jon Stein
Edited by Brian Earnest

Printed in the United States of America

To my wife Tami and son Jared, the loves of my life.

Contents

Introduction

ITARTED MY "EDUCATION" IN CARS by serving as an apprentice for a shop that restored high-point show cars. Every nut and bolt had to be perfect. Every aspect of the car was restored so it resembled a time capsule. You literally stepped back in time to see a car exactly the way it would have rolled off the assembly line. I spent years perfecting my craft and even branched off and ran my own shop. I attended and lectured at many shows, but there always seemed to be something missing.

Somewhere towards the end of the last millennium I found myself speaking in front of a crowd that was mostly full of street rod and custom car enthusiasts. Naturally, the group could really care less about what kind of trivial stamping was found on the head of some bolt. They were mostly interested in what new techniques I offered in the world of paint, but this group rubbed off on me. For the first time in years I felt relaxed at a car show and that's when it hit me: This car show was different. When I came home, I found myself dwelling on the event and my friends were asking me what was different about the show. I guess if I had to summarize the street rod

and custom car world in one word, it would have to be "fun."

The cars are fun and the people are fun, but there is a lot more. Everybody at the show is there to have a good time. It's relaxing. It's creative. There are no boundaries. If you feel like painting the grille and bumpers, go ahead, do it. What's stopping you? There really aren't any rules. Everything is an opinion or personal taste and I love the freedom of custom cars.

Don't believe what you see from Hollywood when it comes to street rods. There are several movies that include old cars in the plot, and the stories are very similar: the main character is somehow an outcast, he finds an old car in a field, spends a couple of weekends working real hard, wipes the grease off his forehead and wins the heart of the most beautiful girl in town. The building of the car usually takes five minutes of the movie or so and gives the impression that building cars is easy and can be done quickly.

Did you ever see the movie "Christine?" I'm the worst one to take to a movie like that because I'm the knucklehead in the back row screaming, "Hey, where did he paint that thing anyway?" "Hey, how did some high school kid pay for the chrome?" Cars take time, so if you are still thinking that you are going to buy this old car in the field, put about 40 hours of hard work into it and sell the car for a profit, then I hope this book will provide a dose of reality. It doesn't happen that way with point show cars and it most certainly doesn't happen with custom cars.

More than anything, I hope this book will help you plan. The lack of a good plan is the most common reason for failed projects. It's the reason why you see so many ads where people are selling unfinished cars. "Must sell—90 percent complete—like new—rare find!" This failure can be avoided with a well-thought-out plan.

The second reason for failure is unrealistic expectations. The first example that comes to mind is the whole 40-hour "Hollywood" thing. It just doesn't happen that way. You should expect to commit 1,000 to 2,000 hours on a custom project, and that takes years, not weeks.

This hobby also takes money, but you do have control over how much. This book will talk about how to set a budget and then plan towards that budget. No high school kid is going to lay down a show car in six weeks working minimum wage and 10 hours a week. It just isn't possible!

Another bubble that I need to burst is the whole myth that you're going to sell this car for a profit and quit your day job. You're just going to have to trust me at this point, but custom automotive work at best will only be worth the sum of its parts.

The very definition of custom car means that this car is special to YOU. The probability that someone will desire every exact detail that matched your personal desires is very low, which means the car's greatest value lies with you. No need to beat a dead horse here, but stick to coin collecting if you're into the money. Continue in your journey with custom cars if you simply love old cars like I do. You wouldn't go to a theme park expecting to make a profit would you? The money is something you pay for the fun!

Safety! OK, Mrs. Fort, my old English teacher, wouldn't approve of me writing a one-word sentence, but safety is very important. I'm going to discuss a whole bunch of really cool, destructive tools. I can relate to the whole "Home Improvement" TV show. I love loud tools that tear stuff up, but you don't have to be missing fingers or have a dog with a patch over its eye to be cool.

I've worked with people with missing eyes and fingers. Cars fall off blocks, too. A friend of the family is no longer with us because he was under a car when it happened, and he left his widow six kids to support. Then there is all the slow agonizing stuff like only having one lung or cancer of the liver. We use a lot of chemicals in this hobby and they require special care to use. Once again, I'm not trying to discourage you, but safety procedures are very important. If someone has experience at something, it doesn't mean that they are good, it just means that they have learned from a lot of mistakes. It's the gruesome mistakes you really want to avoid.

Finally, one of the most exciting aspects of this book, hopefully, is that you will be exposed to a lot of good information. There are numerous resources for parts in the back of this book. At your fingertips will be countless contacts for parts and labor. If you're not on the Internet by now, take the leap of faith and get there. The Web can be perhaps the most important single ally for the automotive enthusiast. I can find a part in hours in what used to take me months. It's awesome!

However, what I am most excited about is something I don't think I have ever seen in a book like this. I have interviewed dozens of established experts in the street rod and custom world and have condensed their knowledge into the pages of this book. We'll drift from shop to shop around the country and see how mechanics and body men tackle problems differently. There will be times where there really isn't a right way to do something and instead of being exposed to just one point of view, we'll see several angles.

This book will hopefully save you time, money and headaches. Hot rodding is a world with no boundaries. I'm really excited, and I hope you are, too.

The Quadracycle was the first vehicle built by automobile pioneer Henry Ford. The year was 1886. *(Henry Ford Museum)*

Chapter 1

How Did Hot Rodding Begin?

I REMEMBER WANDERING THE HALLS of a hot rod show at the Astrodome in Houston, Texas, one summer. As I gazed at the hundreds of cars around me, I couldn't help but wonder: "How and where did this phenomenon begin? Who was responsible? Who built the first hot rod and why?" It turns out the answer is a little complicated.

Many events were involved in the evolution of the modern hot rod. The first was the invention of the automobile itself, and there were many inventors involved in its creation. "Cars" can be traced all the way back to the early 1800s. Actually, they were massive, steam-driven monsters that looked more like large tractors than cars. They weren't even close to practical and were so heavy they would bog down in the crude dirt roads of the time.

Ever heard of a Stanley Steamer? Well, the Stanley brothers were building steam-powered cars as late as the 1920s. Steam engines were big, heavy and difficult to maintain. A new power plant was needed to make cars more practical and we have Nicolaus Otto to thank for it. He invented and built the first four-stroke internal combustion engine and called it the "Otto Cycle Engine." He didn't have it long before he stuck it on a bicycle and made one of the world's first practical motorcycles.

Americans take a lot of pride in their inventions, and there have been many. I seem to recall being told in grade school that Henry Ford invented the first automobile and that Americans were responsible for bringing cars to the world, but that's not really true. Ford was both instrumental and fundamental to the hot rod industry, but he did not invent the car. Essentially, there were hundreds, if not thousands, of inventors all over the world tinkering around

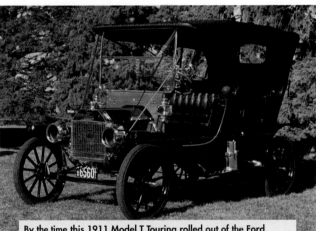

By the time this 1911 Model T Touring rolled out of the Ford factory, the company had already begun to automate its operations and establish itself as an industry leader.

with engines, bicycles and carriages. Many of these people were oceans apart and working on the same invention simultaneously. Usually they were unaware of what the others were doing.

Once upon a time...

Generally, historians look to the person who filed the first patent to be the inventor. If that is the case, the first person to file a patent for a gas-fueled car was German Karl Benz in 1886. His car really looked like a large, three-wheeled motorcycle. So if you ever broke your arm on a three-wheeler as a kid, you have Benz to thank for it. By 1900, his company, Benz & Cie, was the largest manufacturer of automobiles in the world.

The first American inventor of the gas-powered engine was John Lambert in 1891—two years before

The legendary Model T earned its reputation as the first true car of the masses. It was simple, reliable and affordable.

A future hot rod? Some of its contemporaries from 1923 may have wound up modified and "rodded," but this '23 Model T Roadster is a survivor that has changed little from its first day on the road.

Henry Ford. Ford was working for Thomas Edison at the time, but started tinkering with engines and in 1893 he successfully built his first engine, and he ran tested it in the kitchen sink! His wife must have been a tolerant woman, because something tells me he didn't have a muffler on that thing.

His neighbors called him "Crazy Henry" for what appeared to be an obsession with the horseless carriage. Ford worked a normal job for Thomas Edison by day and labored by night in his shed. He was truly a man possessed by his creativity, and in the middle of the night in June of 1896, he finished his first car. There was just one problem: He was so focused on the day-to-day building of the car, that he never bothered to check if it would even fit out the door of his shed. Sure enough, it was too wide. No problem for Ford, however, he just grabbed a sledgehammer and "made" the door wider. Can you see him at 2 in the morning, bashing a hole in the wall of his shed?

By 1901, Ransom Olds made the first real bid to mass produce automobiles, but his car was too fragile and never really caught on. There were at least 30 American auto manufacturers at the turn of the century when some of the first "hot rodding" took place. Cars were still thought of as "freakish" and manufacturers sought out racing as a means to prove roadworthiness to potential customers and pick up some free publicity. However, Ford was a racer before he was a businessman and was actively building race cars by the end of the 19th century. In 1901, he entered one of them in a race at Grosse Pointe, Michigan, and won. This win caught the eye of an investor and together they formed the Ford Motor Company in 1903.

It was the years between 1903-1908 that the

foundation for hot rodding was built. I know that most people in the industry will say hot rodding got started after WWII on a salt flat, but that is just too simplistic.

The earliest hot rods were certainly not the fancy, highly buffed, pretty cars they are today. They were speed machines built on tight budgets, and these mechanics never would have had access to inexpensive parts if it wasn't for Ford and the ideas coming out of his company at this point in history. During the early years, Ford battled with stockholders for the direction of the company. The company first built expensive, highly profitable cars. This may have made the stockholders happy, but he insisted that the future lay with an inexpensive, high-volume solution.

The Ford revolution

If things hadn't changed, we may never have seen the rise of the Ford Company, but a little luck was about to shine on Henry Ford. First, his partner and primary investor ran into financial trouble, which eventually allowed Ford to gain a majority share of stock in his company. Once he had control of the stock he was able to carry out his own ideas. The second event that worked in Ford's favor was an economic crash in 1907. The downward trend in the economy helped convince many stockholders to give Ford's ideas a try. Ford had been pressing for inexpensive, low-margin cars all along, but without these "lucky" events, it's possible Ford would have disappeared with so many other manufacturers in the Great Depression of the 1930s.

Prior to 1908, cars were hand built and produced in small numbers. They were expensive and unreliable, and not considered by most to be a replacement for the horse. Instead, cars were toys or gadgets for the idle rich. Many people who owned cars actually had a full-time mechanic on the payroll and usually drove their cars with the mechanic by their side. It was just easier to use a horse.

Ford's Model T was different. He sat down and designed a car with newer, simplified parts. The cars were reliable, inexpensive to produce and had a simple design that was easy to put together (and easy to take apart—hint, hint). The Model T was also the first American car to use a new kind of steel called vanadium steel (invented by the French). This new steel was lighter and stronger than any other in its time.

Ford kept the options and the choices to a minimum and finally put the build process on an assembly line. All of this controlled costs and led to a low-cost automotive solution that was somewhat reliable. Ford designed the Model T in secret with only a select few of the employees even knowing it existed. One could argue that this was done to avoid industrial espionage, but the more likely reason was to avoid headaches from investors and board members.

It took Ford two years to design, but in 1908, he revealed to the world his little black Model T and asked $850 for it. The car initially was not built on an assembly line, however; it was built in little workstations where a small team of workers put the entire cars together. Ford sold a staggering 10,000 Model T's in its first year. In 1912, the Model T price was reduced to $575 and, for the first time in history, the automobile actually was less than the average annual U.S. wage. By 1913, the process changed so the entire car was built on a conveyer and the first complete automotive assembly line was born. The price quickly dropped to $290 over the next few years.

Henry Ford employed some rather ingenious marketing methods. One of the more humorous was a tour of Model T rodeos where drivers riding in Fords tried to rope cattle. Fords were actually winning endurance races around the country, including the first transcontinental race of 1909. Ford was able to capture the publicity of the win, even though his modified Model T was later disqualified when officials learned that the engine was changed during the race. Either way, only three cars actually finished the race and two of those were modified Model T's. Ford's reliability proved to be a powerful marketing tool and the word was spreading that these Model T's could someday replace the horse!

Ford is generally credited with implementing the first assembly line, which led to mass production. Actually, he borrowed the assembly line idea after he took a trip to Chicago once and toured the famous Chicago meat-packing plants. The beef carcasses would travel on an overhead trolley and each butcher would remove their specific cut of beef and push the carcass on to the next butcher. In effect, this was a non-motorized "disassembly" line.

Ford started introducing automation in his factory in 1910 and tinkered with it every day. The task before him was staggering. No two portions of a car take the exact same time to build. Take the chassis for example. The frames would have to be put in jigs and riveted or welded together, then passed on to the next station. There, a worker would add the first foundation parts, like suspension, and then pass it on. This would continue until there was a finished chassis and it would pass on down the line for body assembly.

The problem that Ford had to tackle concerned the timing of the line. For example, it's a lot easier and faster to bolt leaf springs on a frame than it is to build the frame itself, so you ended up with some workers sitting around waiting for the next task. He eventually solved this problem with trial and error, old-fashioned hard work and sheer genius.

By the time the Model A arrived, the early Model T's had begun to collect dust and rust in backyards around the country.

The Model A arrived on the scene in 1928 and made the long-running Model T obsolete. It also made them candidates to be turned into backroad racers by backyard mechanics looking for a little amusement. (Jim Dunn)

Make way for the Model A

OK, so what does all this history stuff have to do with hot rods? Well, Henry Ford and his company were so efficient that by 1927, 15 million Model T's had been produced, which represented half of the cars in existence at the time. Trouble had been brewing, though. Chevrolet had been steadily eroding Model T sales. Drivers could get more amenities for a similar low price and the writing was on the wall that the Model T needed to be changed. Henry Ford would hear nothing of it and insisted the Model T was here to stay. It took the constant nagging of his son and a rapid drop in sales in 1927 to convince him otherwise.

Ford then provided an example of what not to do when transitioning a factory to something new. Ford quickly decided that a new model was needed, so he shut down the plant and sent all the workers home for six months! He and his team of engineers designed the new model and ramped up the assembly line for the next great thing—the Model A. Keep in mind, there was no vast network of used car sales at the time. Many people just kept the old T's as a second car or retired them to a barn.

At this point in history, America was in an economic boom, with 15 million Model T's on the roads and a brand-new model essentially making all of these older cars obsolete. Several million

more Model A's were produced in just the four years between 1928 and 1932. If you include all the manufacturers, there were more than 30 million obsolete cars floating around the country with no real resale value.

The U.S. government actually considered this a great problem. The great stock market crash of 1929 led to a massive depression and new car sales plummeted. In the years that followed, the majority of America's several hundred auto manufacturers either went out of business or merged with each other due to low sales volume. Many of the Model T cars were built so well that they were still running well into the 1930s, so many Americans opted to hold off on buying a new car until things got better. The U.S. government decided that the solution to ending the Depression was to get people to buy goods again, so the government started destroying huge surpluses of goods in the hopes that it would force people to buy things again.

Most of the destruction centered on agriculture, but cars were not immune. There are numerous photos of tall Model T bonfires. Of course, no recycling was authorized. The goal of this exercise was to get manufacturers to buy new steel, too. The photos are somewhat disturbing for car lovers, but the good news is that there were so many cars produced that the government didn't come close to making a dent in the surplus of old cars. If they had, the story of the hot rod would have been much different.

Picking up speed

By 1932, advanced technology was on the way, like the V-8 engine. Car manufacturers started boasting claims of stock car speeds in excess of 70 mph! America began to feel a need for speed. It's difficult to say who built the first hot rod. One could argue that those 1901 speedsters Henry Ford raced on were hot rods, but a more accepted definition for hot rod is "any pre-1949 car that has been modified to gain speed."

If you have an interest in early hot rod history, I highly recommend reading the book *Hot Rod Magazine: The First 12 Issues.*" Several clues to the origin of hot rods can be found in these first issues of the magazine. The majority of the photos center on oval track racing and not the speed records of the Bonneville Salt Flats. Another interesting note of the early years can be found in the ads themselves. You don't find the term "hot rod" used in the commercial ads. Instead, you see the term "speed" used where we use the term custom or street rod today. Many of the advertisements feature "speed shops" or "speed parts."

Early hot rodding was not about *American Graffiti* Saturday night cruising or fancy car shows, but more about racing and setting land speed records. Of course, no magazine would be complete without a "Hot Rod of the Month" page or pictures of women posing with car parts. It had a *Playboy* feel about it, even though it was a good six years before that magazine came along. Most of the cars are not painted, and are very rough by today's standards. However, one thing is clear: By the time the magazine was first issued in 1948, a whole hot rodding industry already existed.

Born on the back roads

So when did hot rods first hit the streets and why? Well, we have to take a guess at the why, but there are pictures of crude hot rods all the way back to the '30s. Our best guess of the "why" revolves around friendship and competition. It's likely that the first hot rods were only slightly modified and were used as a low-cost source of entertainment for young men around the country.

Picture this scenario: Two pals from high school have several things in common. Their parents both have 20-year-old Model T's sitting in the barn collecting dust, both have limited budgets and both have free time on their hands after school and chores. Every weekend these pals would race around the rural dirt roads of the day and every week each would learn some new trick. It wasn't long before engine modifications were being made and excess sheet metal was removed to pick up extra speed. This scenario was not unusual. After all, some locations around the country didn't have electricity, let alone movie theaters or other forms of entertainment. Amateur racing was fun and people all over the country were discovering it. As more people got involved in the "speed" hobby, small dirt tracks were built to provide a safe place for people to race.

Why spend so much time discussing Henry Ford? Well, by the 1930s you had millions of aging, obsolete and "extra" vehicles around just waiting to be tinkered with. The extra cars were a great source of cheap parts, too. By the time World War II started, the hot rod industry had already set roots, but soon everyone, both male and female, had a job to do and there wasn't much extra time to tinker with hot rods. Even though the war may have put a halt to hot rodding initially, it actually added fuel to the fire. You almost couldn't be involved in that war without picking up some mechanical skills.

Many observers have said that the war was won by the mobility the jeep offered. If you were in a tank, jeep or truck that broke down, you couldn't pull over to the side of the road and wait for a wrecker. It was in a soldier's best interest to pick up a few mechanical skills and get their vehicle going themselves.

By 1946, most Americans had been deprived of a new car for four years or more, so the demand for new vehicles skyrocketed after the war. A surge of postwar car buying began, which resulted in the retirement of all the '30s coupes and sedans. Remember all of those factory claims of 70-mph stock coupes? What would happen if we took one of those old cars, hopped up the engine, beefed up the suspension and shed some extra weight? All we needed were those extra, now inexpensive V-8 engines to complete the puzzle.

With the arrival of full-blown mass production, there were literally millions of scrap vehicles available for parts at near "giveaway" prices. We had road tracks for safe racing peppered all over the country and new ones were being built all the time. There was a surplus of powerful engines that were easy to work on and a nation full of young mechanics looking for something to do. The growth of the hot rod was inevitable.

Chapter 2

Developing a Plan

Classic cars appeal to the masses, but many people want a classic look with a more reliable or smoother ride. A semi-modified hot rod like this 1953 Buick may be the answer.

NOW I DON'T WANT TO COME ACROSS like I'm giving a father-in-law speech, but perhaps the most important question I could ask any prospective hot rodder or custom car builder is "What is your plan?" When I read books, I'm bad about skipping the introduction; and if some of you have the same bad habits, you may have missed a very important point: Don't even pick up a wrench without having a plan! If you already started a project and don't have a clear vision of where you're going, then stop!

The simple truth is this: The primary reason for failed custom projects is a lack of planning.

So where do we start? Well, we'll begin with the most obvious question first: What kind of custom car are we going to build? I give lectures and seminars at trade shows. After the presentations, I can't tell you how many people come up to ask questions and their entire plan is sketched out on a napkin! "And ... you already mailed out checks and started spreading your credit card around buying parts with this? This napkin is your plan?" Sometimes in all the excitement, we get ahead of ourselves.

So many people start with a sketch or a picture of what the car will look like and start picking color options from day one with no plan. Have you set a budget? Do you know how much time you will spend on this? How much will you do yourself?

This is an "over the top" version of an all-time classic. Hot rods have their roots in the Model T. America's first rods were stripped down T's. However, this one may get a little hairy when that blower opens up!

What kind of car?

Your plan should include a folder of information, and your first step is choosing the car's style. This is an important step and some serious thought should go into this. Study all the different styles, address their difficulty, and discuss how expensive they are to build. Let's start this process with the cars that are the easiest and least expensive to build and work up.

The cars that come first are actually the ones that come first in hot rodding history. This makes sense because these first hot rods were built on low budgets by pioneers of the industry. The first two types of hot rods were roadsters and streamliners. Both of these are cool-looking cars that are fairly easy to build and are great beginner cars.

Roadsters

The traditional roadster was generally a '20s or '30s Ford that had all the unnecessary sheet metal removed and improvements made to the engine and suspension. They were almost always open cars with no roof, fenders or engine cowl. Many of them had Model T bodies with nothing but the radiator out front. This was the easiest car to build and is

Big, heavy custom cars of the 1950s and early 1960s are often referred to as lead sleds, kustoms, or customs. These cars are huge, require a lot of bodywork, have a lot of parts and factory options, and can be very expensive to tackle as a street rod project. This 1949 Caddy has a beautiful paint job and flawless bodywork.

the most common car you see in the old issues of *Hot Rod Magazine*. These first cars were not exactly attractive in the sense the interiors were stripped and they lacked paint, but they were usually fast. In today's market, you would expect this type of car to have both beautiful paint and interior work along with several other modern amenities, like fuel injection, disc brakes and stereo equipment.

This style of car is frequently what comes to mind when people think of a "hot rod," but it could also be called a "high boy" or "street rod." A very nice version of this can be built on a budget of $20,000, with that

The "T-Bucket" roadster is the ultimate old school hot rod. Topless, fenderless and hoodless may not be the most practical way to go, but for many the T-Bucket is the ultimate street rod.

price coming down if you do more work yourself. I highly recommend that your first car fall into this category. This may not be what you sketched on that napkin, but it's a good idea to start with something simple and work your way up as you learn.

Streamliners

The other type of early hot rod was called the "streamliner," and this style is very rare today. This was essentially a race car with sheet metal wrapped around the driver and enclosing the engine compartment to reduce drag. Sometimes mechanics would build these out of old drop tanks from WWII fighters and most of the first speed records were made in streamliners. The problem with them is they only seat one person, which is fine for racing but isn't exactly fun on a Saturday night. I guess a modern equivalent would be today's Formula 1 and Indy cars. Since streamliners are not exactly practical, I will be spending very little time talking about building them.

"Street rods"

"Street rod" is a newer term and it covers any custom car built before 1949. The definition is similar to hot rod and most people use the terms interchangeably. There are some hot rod clubs that are Ford specific, but street rod clubs are all encompassing and welcome all makes. You would expect to see some roadsters and high boys at a street rod show, but the majority of the cars are enclosed with a chopped roof and have most of their original sheet metal, like the fenders and hood. They usually have the trim and bumpers removed with an array of paint schemes and interior styles. This is very much a free-form vehicle built with an "anything goes" approach. Street rods usually have an intact body that seats four and are not much more difficult to build than the hot rod roadsters.

Their cost varies from the same $20,000 to outrageous, depending on the modifications made. Typically the national show winners have a good $150,000 in them and tour the national show circuit. The shows generally require some kind of display and most of these cars travel in a full-length tractor-trailer rig. You can build a very nice street rod in the $20,000 to $40,000 price range.

"Custom" cruisers

Every car mentioned so far is a custom car. Custom only implies that changes have been made

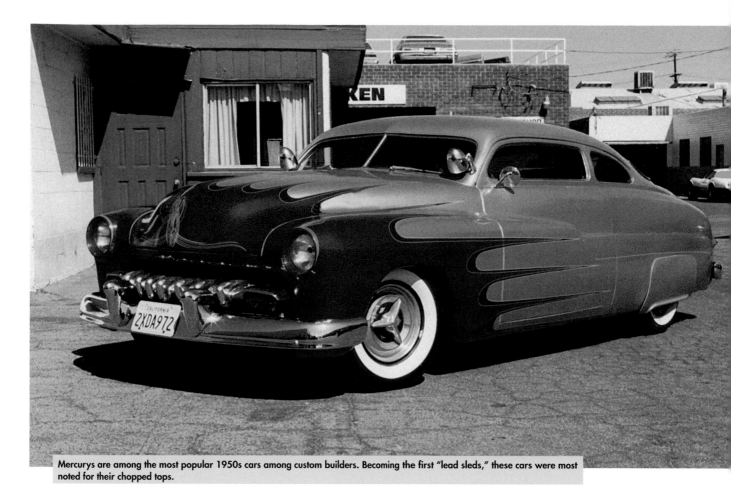

Mercurys are among the most popular 1950s cars among custom builders. Becoming the first "lead sleds," these cars were most noted for their chopped tops.

to alter the car from stock. The term "custom" is used for everything under the sun. However, when I hear the term "custom," I usually think of a '50s or '60s car built for cruising. After all, if the hot rod industry got started to fulfill the need for speed, the custom or "kustom" industry began to express individuality. Most people in the industry have then taken the word "kustom" to describe this era of Saturday night cruisers. These cars are large, heavy, time consuming and fairly costly to build.

One type of custom car is a modified or semi-modified style. These cars are essentially stock with just a few changes. I won't spend a lot of time addressing this class of vehicle because they do not have much customization. I recommend staying 100 percent original or going full custom. A stock car with one change, like mag wheels, often just looks odd.

The lead sled

Custom cars include the "lead sled" varieties. Custom cars hit the scene in the late 1940s and '50s and many of the people involved were hot rodders. Some people enjoyed working on cars but just didn't have an interest in racing. Many of the first custom techniques involved paint. I

have always thought that flames came first and scallops followed decades later, but I have now seen examples of simple scallop designs back in the '40s, which leads me to believe scallops came first and morphed into flames during the '50s. Every time someone thought of something new like candied paint or flames, it wasn't long before everyone was following suit, so people looked at the body itself to find originality.

Some of the first modifications centered on cleaning the factory-built lines. Bumpers, mirrors, door handles and chrome decorations came off. It wasn't until people started grafting the parts from one car into another before the "lead sled" came into the picture. Whenever you take an external part, like a taillight, and sink it into the body so it fits flush, you have a process called "frenching." Frenched lights give the car a very sleek, clean appearance, but require welding on the skin of the body to pull off properly.

In the '40s and '50s, you didn't have polyester fillers like Bondo available, so people used lead to fill in the welds and low spots. By the time you french in all the exterior parts, chop the top, and even modify the shape of the body; you end up with quite a bit of lead on the car and hence the term "lead sled."

Rat rods are making their mark on the hot rodding circuit. Either flat black or not painted at all, these cars are throwbacks to the original hot rodding era.

The welding seams of this rat are clearly visible. Notice the holes cut out of the frame. The money invested in this car has been almost entirely devoted to speed.

Rat rods

Rat rods are a fairly new fad that sort of took off in the mid 1990s. They are essentially the original hot rods, but have taken on a whole new meaning. High-end hot rodding has definitely become a hobby for the wealthy. The cars that win shows are usually $100,000-plus trailer queens. The rats are a throwback to a time where speed, not looks, was what counted.

A rat rod is any hot rod where the minimum was spent to get speed. In addition, the rats seem to go out of their way to be as ugly as possible. Many aren't even painted, and some are rusty hulks. Exposed and rusty welds are commonplace, but the engine remains choice. As a whole, hot rodders are thumbing their noses at these ugly ducklings, but I think they are important. A hobby shouldn't be just for the wealthy! There's room for all in the hot rodding world.

Lowering and channeling

Some customizers were not satisfied with the height of their cruiser, so they looked for ways to lower the car to the ground. The first efforts at this involved cutting links out of the front coil springs and removing leafs out of the rear, but this decreased performance and proved dangerous in some cases. Along comes channeling. Channeling can be time consuming; but what happens is the customizer removes the metal on the floor that is in contact with the frame, lowers the body in relation to the ground and welds the floor back up. Frenching and channeling are not tasks for the novice. They are time consuming, and in this business, time equals big money.

Theme

Theme is a newer focus to hot rodding. When fiberglass shops began reproducing popular body

Theme has become an integral part of hot rod culture. Originally a focus of only show cars, theme is what now sets a car apart from the rest. Thousands of identical fiberglass bodies are stamped out each year, and a little extra effort is needed to bring originality back to fiberglass rods. This one has a Hawaiian theme.

styles like the '32 coupe, numerous rodders ended up with nearly identical cars. This is most evident at the larger shows where several thousand rods from around the country end up in one place. How many times can you change the color of the same car before things get dull?

Theme goes farther than paint and interior design. The theme is a detailed idea or feeling that continues all around the car from top to bottom. In the past, flames were detail added to the outside of the hood and fenders. Now, the theme would take those flames and extend them to the interior and under the hood. Components may be carved out of billet aluminum into flames and small details may be added all over the car. The flames may be added to the frame or maybe the instruments light up as flames on the dash. The more creative and detailed the theme, the better.

However, the ideas for the theme may be easier to come by than the money to pay for them. The more intricate the theme, the more expensive the project will likely be. It's important to budget for, and to understand, what the theme items will be before you start. For example, you may want to eliminate metal trim and go with a rather unique painted-on trim. This is not a decision that can be made late

The flower pattern extends around the beltline and into the interior. Note the continuation of the leaf from the door jam onto the dash.

The flowers continue under the hood. Details like this surfboard, theme paint and modest chrome set the engine compartment off nicely.

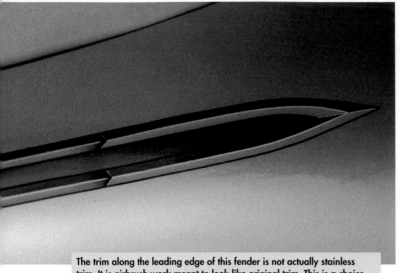

The trim along the leading edge of this fender is not actually stainless trim. It is airbrush work meant to look like original trim. This is a choice, but one that needs to be made early, because original holes will have to be welded up and bodywork needed before paint is applied.

Like trim, emblems can be painted on as well. *(Street Rods by Michael)*

Sometimes it is easier to visualize the final product with a professional sketch. This same body can be manipulated over and over with different color combinations until you have found the one you want. Grilles, wheels, interiors and trim can all easily be changed. *(Zombie)*

into the process as traditional trim mounting holes have to be welded up and smoothed over in the bodywork phase. Some theme items can be relatively inexpensive to produce. A constant paint theme throughout the car, or even the addition of small personal items like dice, can contribute to the theme without adding significantly to the cost.

Theme is all the rage and will most likely continue far into the future. Try to find a way to develop a theme that is both personable and affordable. Once, I saw a car that had small religious scriptures painted on it. Although religion is not a normal theme element, it told me something about the owner that I might not have otherwise known.

What is your passion outside of rodding? That may be your perfect theme element.

Can startup drawings help?

Absolutely! There is no overstating the importance of a comprehensive plan. Drawings and colored sketches are important and can save you big bucks later on. They will be most useful when you get to the paint and upholstery phase.

By all means, if you have artistry skills, sketch your heart out. Often this is the "dreaming" phase

Coca-Cola is the obvious theme here. The custom trailer is an interesting addition to the overall picture.

Often the theme revolves around miniatures. Look carefully inside this panel truck and you will see a toy replica. Other rodders will have pedal cars made out to look just like their ride.

The late Ed "Big Daddy" Roth remains a huge influence on the hot rod community. You will see tributes to Ed at almost any show you go to. Rat Fink was one of his most famous characters.

Continuation of theme in the engine compartment is almost required these days for show cars. A lot of hours can be spent manufacturing the custom sheet metal needed to pull off this look, but the end result is super clean.

This paint scheme wraps around nicely into the engine area. Theme-oriented paint can be seen on the air scoop and valve covers. This is a nice changeup to the overdone chrome look of the past. Also of interest is the super clean, custom firewall.

that provokes creativity. Even though most of us can draw the outline of a car, detailed and scaled drawings will be the ones needed. Most of us just can't draw that well. That is where a professional artist like Zombie comes in. Zombie is in tune to the rodding industry and can translate your ideas into feasible designs.

A professional artist like this can finalize your idea into a black-and-white sketch. He can then manipulate that sketch into a multitude of color and graphic schemes without damaging the original concept. This allows you to explore different ideas in an affordable way. Check out his Web site at http://www.zombiehotrodwear.com.

Budgeting

Proper budgeting is key to a good plan and as I walk you through the steps in the next chapters, I will point out what certain parts and labor cost. I recommend that you set a budget first, read the chapters thoroughly and then decide what you will need to do to stick to your budget.

For example, if you set a budget for $10,000, a car can still be made, but you will need to learn almost every skill involved, including all mechanical, body, paint and interior work. To pull it off, you'll be getting parts out of junkyards, painting parts instead

of chroming them, painting the car in your garage and stitching the interior yourself. I have been doing this for years and still wouldn't try to do everything myself. Being realistic with your skills assessment also leads to a good plan and a higher probability of success. Building a nice street rod for less than $15,000 is not easy to do.

The good news is that this is the very definition of planning. Read the entire book, select the type of custom car you like, budget the parts, materials and labor, and methodically act out your plan step by step. You do as much work as you feel comfortable with and get a professional to do the rest. I highly recommend surfing the Web and looking at the endless supply of custom car photos. Thousands of people have posted their e-mail addresses online and you can start networking with people who have been down the same road. Keep a folder with all your contacts and start pricing parts and asking questions. Once this research folder is complete, you can consider putting money into your rod.

One page on Michael Young's Web site is extremely helpful during planning: http://www.srbymichael.com/arc.shtml. I recommend visiting this site and looking for a car you like. The site breaks down more than a dozen models by price. The following is one example found on this site. Your plan should include a price breakout similar to this one.

Street Rods by Michael

Redneck '32 3W Hi-Boy ARC

Body: Redneck '32 3-window coupe, stock top

Features: Stock height top, doors hung with stock hinges, door latches installed, deck lid mounted, dash installed, defroster ducts installed, garnish moldings.

Body price	$8,500
Downs Manufacturing Trunk Lift	▲ $250

Options

Power windows installed	$850
Dash extender	▲ $135
Upholstery Package	▲ $500
Tinted front glass	$200
Head lights, bar, conduit, w/pads & bolts	$279
Parking & turn signal lights	▲ $20
Specialty wipers w/intermediate	▲ $300
Taillights pair—'39 Ford blue dot w/pads	▲ $78
Grille shell & insert	$435
Alumicraft grille Insert (⅜ inch spacing, front polished)	▲ $170
Hood: 3- or 4-piece complete (scoops or louvers option)	$550
Hood prop, bars, brackets bumper kit & center—4-piece hood only	▲ $111
Outside handles (door & deck lid)	▲ $82
Weatherstrip kit	▲ $95
Wipers installed	▲ $225
TOTAL (base)	**$10,814**

Frame

Features: Fully boxed frame—front & rear crossmember, tube center manual brake pedal assembly and master cylinder—Vega mount, complete 4 bar front end or hair pin with axle, spring, spring perches, spring shackles, steering arms, spindles, shocks, u-bolt, lower shock mounts, king pins, tie rod with ends, brackets welded in place, front brake kit, drag link, pitman arm, front panhard bar, Vega steering box, Ford 9-inch rear end housing narrowed with axles, bearings, rear brakes, backing plates, third member rebuilt (275,300,325), rear coil over shocks, triangular 4 bar or parallel 4 bar*, all brackets welded in place
*Parallel 4 bar need rear panhard bar—see Options below for price

Stage 3 chassis, complete	$6,895
C notch rear	▲ $110
Notch front	▲ $75
Bob rear of frame	▲ $75
Pro street	▲ $600
Chrome front axle w/GM brakes, front spring and shocks	▲ $800
Plain drilled I beam w/GM brakes, front spring and shocks	▲ $150
Chrome drilled I beam w/GM brakes, front spring and shocks	▲ $850
Super Deluxe Chrome Package—Wilwood Brakes, finned backing plates.	▲ $1,620

▲ Denotes upgrade price

This is a higher-end version of the parts list below. This high boy includes most upgrade options as well as a $10,000-plus engine package. *(Gibbon Fiberglass Reproductions)*

IFS standard—GM brakes	▲ $275
IFS SS—GM brakes, includes rear 4-bar upgrade to chrome	▲ $1,150
IFS show custom disc brakes incl rear 4-bar upgrade to chrome	▲ $1,400
IFS show 12-inch drilled disc polished 4-piston caliper, incl 4-bar upgrade chrome	▲ $1,900
IFS show 13-inch drilled disc polished 6-piston caliper, including 4-bar upgrade chrome	▲ $2,570
Rear tri 4-bar chrome and polished shocks	▲ $160
Rear tri 4-bar chrome, polished shocks and chrome springs	▲ $285
Rear panhard bar when using parallel 4-bar	▲ $100
Rear chrome panhard bar when using parallel 4-bar	▲ $136
SVO Ford rear disc brakes	▲ $159
Wilwood polished rear disc with internal e-brake	▲ $575
Power brakes w/master cylinder & booster—plain	▲ $200
Power brakes w/master cylinder & booster—chrome	▲ $268
Steel brake lines w/residual valves & proportionate valve	▲ $450
SS brake lines w/residual valves & proportionate valve	▲ $350
Drive shaft	▲ $300
Emergency brake, cables, & boot—Lokar	▲ $209
Fuel lines	$50
Poly tank w/cover, tanks	$285
Gas tank, SS Rock Valley	▲ $220
TOTAL (base)	**$7,230**

Engine

Crate engine—SBC 210 hp	$1,700
Crate engine—SBC 300 hp	▲ $1,000
Crate engine—SBC 355 hp	▲ $2,675
Brackets—Alan Grove alternator	$70
Brackets—Billet Specialties polished A/C/Alt.	▲ $150
Pulleys—Chevrolet stock steel pulleys	▲ $100
Pulleys—Billet Specialties V-belt polished	▲ $40
Alternator—100-amp—chrome	▲ $124
Water pump—plain SW	$35
Water pump—Tuff-Stuff chrome SW	▲ $60
Starter—plain	▲ $75
Starter—PowerMaster mini-Chevy chrome	▲ $155
Headers—T'coated	$330
Intake—carburetor (not required with 355 hp)	$175
Carburetor—Holley 650	$325
Electric fuel pump in line	$74
Exhaust system w/mufflers aluminized	$450
Harmonic balancer—not required with 355 hp	$88
Radiator—Griffin aluminum 2 rows 1 1/4 inch tubes	$570
Radiator hoses	$60
Radiator cap	$20
Electric fan—Spal 16-inch & thermostat switch	$150
Spark plugs & wires	$84
Spark plug wire looms	$40
Automotive belts	$30
Distributor (not required with 355 hp)	$250
Coil (not required with 355 hp)	$40
Air cleaner—chrome	▲ $40
Air cleaner—billet	▲ $65
Valve covers & breathers (2)—Billet	$160
Throttle cable, kickdown, bracket & spring—Lokar	$115
Water neck	$30
Engine & transmission dipsticks—Lokar	$107
Oil, transmission fluid, anti-freeze	$46
Battery, cables, eyes & cut off switch	$225
Wiring harness—18 circuit	▲ $325
TOTAL	**$5,174**

Transmission

Type 350 w/torque converter	$1,200
Type 700R w/torque converter & electrical	▲ $600
Shifter—Lokar—12-inch—350/700R w/boot	$222
Transmission cooler & hoses	$145
Flex plate & bolts (not required with 355 hp)	$65
Transmission dust cover 350/700R	$65
TOTAL (base)	**$1,697**

Accessories

Gauges Dakota Digital w/bezel	▲ $550
Gauges—Classic Inst 5 Gauge Set	▲ $441
Steering column—ididit paintable tilt & drop & floor mount	$482
Steering joints with rod	$247
Steering wheel—LeCarra—Mark 9	$125
Steering wheel adaptor—polished	$69
7 channel remote w/actuators—balls	▲ $310
Door handles—nostalgia inside or door latch knobs	$30
Wheels & lug nuts—American polished torque thrusters	$750
Tires—radials mounted	$300
License plate frame—billet light	$50
Third brake light LED—gearhead	▲ $95
Insulation—Koolmat & bubble foil	▲ $50
Outside mirrors—billet	▲ $120
Rear view mirror—billet	$53
Heat & air conditioning unit—Vintage Air—Gen II Compact	▲ $405
Compressor—plain—Sanden	▲ $200
Compressor—chrome—Sanden	▲ $280
Condensor—Vintage Air	▲ $139
Trinary Switch—Vintage Air	▲ $51
Hose kit & dryer—black—Vintage Air	▲ $100
Hose kit & dryer—chrome—Vintage Air	$179
Gas & brake pedal—Lokar	$120
Switch kit—ignition, light	$65
Miscellaneous	$1,000
TOTAL	**$3,470**

Paint

Paint engine, transmission	▲ $100
Grind, smooth, paint—engine, transmission	▲ $1,200
Grind smooth frame, rear end housing—paint	▲ $1,400
All suspension pieces, MC, brake pedal arm, etc.—powder coat	▲ $400
Paint body, hood, doors, underneath, etc.	▲ $6,000

Interior

Interior cloth (herculon), Glide seats or Tea's Design	▲ $5,500
Leather or any customized interior would be subject to price.	
Convertible top bid from upholster only.	
LABOR TOTAL	**$5,500**
GRAND TOTAL (base)	**$34,585**

(Note: Labor cost may increase with upgrades)

Chapter 3

Metal and Fiberglass Bodies

It's not easy to distinguish a well-done fiberglass body from a metal body when the car is finished.

THERE ARE TWO WAYS TO GO when it comes to hot rod car bodies—metal or fiberglass. The greatest advantage of a steel car is that the body and the frame were made for each other and already fit. Providing that you don't make radical changes, you should feel comfortable that the body will set on the frame nicely. The exact opposite is true for fiberglass bodies. It is very unusual for a fiberglass body to mate to the chassis with no modifications. We will share some tips to make this chore easier; however, it is still a chore.

One reason why professionals prefer metal-bodied projects is that there is a wider variety of body styles to choose from. Fiberglass bodies come from molds, which are time consuming and expensive to manufacture. Therefore, there are far fewer fiberglass styles or bodies to choose from. Early Ford models dominate fiberglass design so much that you can easily end up with an identity crisis. If your car looks just like everyone elses, is it truly a custom? Metal car bodies will give you an endless choice of styles to meld into your creativity. However, metal body modifications and rust repair can be difficult in a hobby environment. Expensive sandblasting, welding, cutting and grinding tools are needed in metal work.

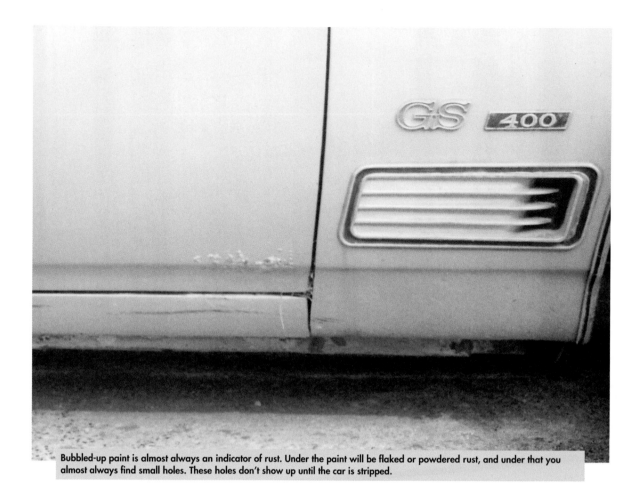

Bubbled-up paint is almost always an indicator of rust. Under the paint will be flaked or powdered rust, and under that you almost always find small holes. These holes don't show up until the car is stripped.

Rust, not design, is usually your greatest adversary in metal bodies. What starts as a small hole usually turns into a headache once the car is stripped. Rust repair can be extremely time consuming. I recall several occasions where I stepped back from a major rust repair, scratched my head and asked, "Was this really worth it? Why did I bother with this one again?"

Although metal-bodied cars are traditional and preferred by most professionals, there are times where fiberglass makes sense. Metal bodies usually have the advantage when it comes to spare parts because they are complete cars. They already have all of the little screws, brackets and hinges that are necessary to build the car. Fiberglass bodies rarely come as kits that include everything you need to assemble the car.

On the other hand, it is very unusual to find a metal car body that is less work than a fiberglass one. Fiberglass bodies come already modified. For example, most '32 coupes will already have some degree of roof chopping incorporated into the design. Other "small" items like trim or decorative mounting holes will already be filled. Of course, these holes have to be welded up on a metal car and

there can be dozens of them. The trick in fiberglass is not dealing with rust, but finding a quality kit at a reasonable price.

The big decision

The choice of the car itself has probably led to more failed restoration and rod attempts than any other. Picking a donor car to start with is an important step in the plan. It is very tempting to draw out a car on a napkin, get really excited and go buy the first thing you see so you can get started as soon as possible. The enthusiasm is wonderful, but remember that you are on a long road. You will win this war through small, tedious battles. Never rush into it.

By the time we go car hunting, we should have a custom style laid out with some rough sketches of what the finished product should look like. We should know the year or years that are acceptable to use, what kind of chassis to use and what modifications will be made. We also should have a rough idea what the interior and exterior will look like, including what exterior trim will be used. Knowing whether we need all the trim moldings and chrome bumpers

Floor pan repair is fairly common for metal bodied cars. Most street rodders tackled this with a flat and simple sheet metal replacement. However, you can still spend at least $1,000 on this routine repair.

is important before we select the donor vehicle.

Above all we should have a budget, not just for the finished project, but also for what we are going to spend for a donor vehicle.

Shopping tips

Most of a street rod or custom car is painted, chromed, removed or modified, so we don't necessarily need a mint-condition original for the donor. As a matter of fact, a mint-condition vehicle is not preferred. You will pay top dollar for one and only dismantle or destroy most of it anyway. What we really need to do is only pay for the critical parts we need.

For example, does the car even need to have an engine? Most people use new power plants in their custom cars. Most people also build custom interiors, so the interior doesn't need to be nice. Some custom builders will design cars that don't need all the sheet metal.

Every builder will have a different plan, so I cannot take you through every specific step, but take a close look at the metal you need. Especially,

look at the inside of the trunk, wheel wells and under the rocker panels or step boards. These areas are notorious for rust. Are there any special parts missing? For instance, if you are looking at a convertible as a donor, does it have the top mechanism, top switch and rear seat? These parts are special to all convertibles and are very difficult to find. If we are using the chrome, it not only needs to be there, but all the steel parts should be straight and the pot metal parts should be void of pits. Both of these problems can force a builder to purchase new parts later down the road. Don't be hesitant to take a magnet with you. Areas with no magnetic pull either have body filler or lead in them, which usually indicates a problem or older patchwork.

Both the fender and wheel well have extensive rust. Although many makes have replacement panels available, the effort to replace both the fender and inner fender well outweighs the value of the car. Problems like this make the car an unwise choice. Fiberglass bodies will be less work, so pass on this and keep looking for the right body.

I recommend getting somewhat picky here. Builders looking at early model street rods have good fiberglass bodies and new frames to fall back on. Custom builders looking at 1940-'60s model custom cars have newer metal and thousands of good cars still on the roads. If the rust holes are larger than 1/4 inch in diameter or the vehicle has been wrecked in any way, pass. There are other choices out there.

The Internet is a wonderful tool. It can save so much time, but I'm horrified every time I hear of people putting deposits down or buying cars without even seeing them. Never buy sight unseen. Take the time to see the car and inspect it with your own eyes. Photographs save time initially, but they only tell a part of the story.

Fiberglass kits

Fiberglass bodies and kits can lead to a whole new nightmare. Many of the kits do not fit together well and require major re-engineering to complete. The details here can kill you.

I recommend a few steps to protect yourself. First, I would not purchase a fiberglass kit unless you have a recommendation from a friend or club member. Let somebody else be the guinea pig. If you meet someone who has built a kit from a specific manufacturer with good results and limited frustration, then by all means use that vendor. I so strongly suggest using that vendor that I would even alter my plan, if necessary, to accommodate the new vendor's spec's.

The second piece of advice is don't just buy a body, look for a whole kit. Someone who has thought the whole kit out has more than likely built his own product and refined it. You would be surprised how many vendors haven't even built their own product before.

Rusted-out areas need to be cut out and replaced. The rear of a car like this can run around $2,000.

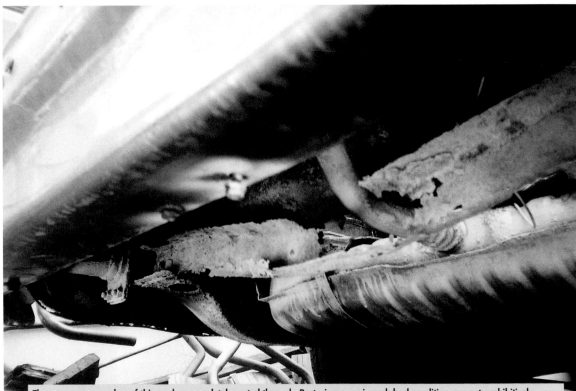

The rear cross member of this car has completely rusted through. Restoring a car in such bad condition can get prohibitively expensive. Look for a better candidate for your custom project.

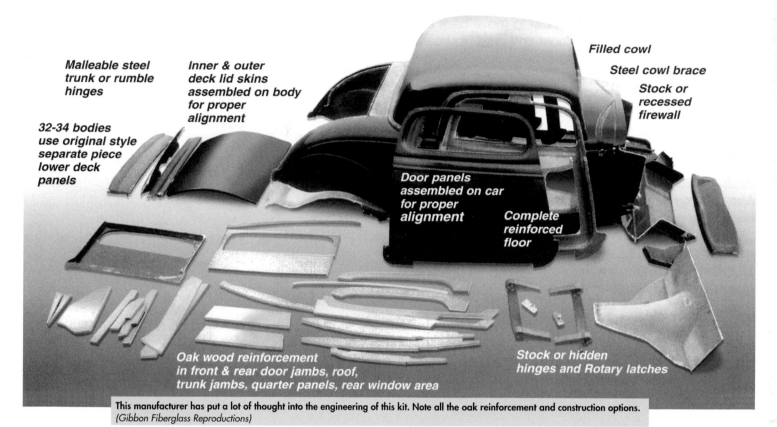

Malleable steel trunk or rumble hinges

Inner & outer deck lid skins assembled on body for proper alignment

Filled cowl

Steel cowl brace

Stock or recessed firewall

32-34 bodies use original style separate piece lower deck panels

Door panels assembled on car for proper alignment

Complete reinforced floor

Oak wood reinforcement in front & rear door jambs, roof, trunk jambs, quarter panels, rear window area

Stock or hidden hinges and Rotary latches

This manufacturer has put a lot of thought into the engineering of this kit. Note all the oak reinforcement and construction options. (Gibbon Fiberglass Reproductions)

Take special interest in the way the kit fits together. How did the manufacturer engineer the door, trunk and hood hinges? I have seen some kits where the hinges screw right into the fiberglass using home door hinges and wood screws! Of course, this is more than likely found on the lowest-priced kits, so keep in mind that you do get what you pay for. Remember, most hinges are hard steel and fiberglass is fairly soft. The two don't go together well and creative engineering is required to solve this problem.

When you are looking for vendors, look for one that offers a kit where the doors, trunk and hood come pre-mounted. Most of the higher-quality vendors offer this service for about $1,000 more,

and it can be worth every cent. Do not be fooled into thinking this is an easy task. I would guess that if a vendor doesn't offer this service, it is a red flag that something is wrong with the kit itself.

Take a close look at how the body is finished. This may mean you have to take a trip to the factory to see the manufacturing process. Ask people who have built the kit questions concerning the amount of time that was needed to get the body straight before painting. Fiberglass bodies have a reputation for being very wavy. The more questions you ask, the better. Remember, you pay for a kit up front and have very few return options. Let the buyer beware when it comes to fiberglass.

Chapter 4

Chassis

Many builders find the chassis-building process one of the most enjoyable parts of a custom build. With the body off the car, the mechanics are easy to see and enjoy. (*Gibbon Fiberglass Reproductions*)

THE MOST COMMON MISTAKE in street rod planning starts out something like this: You know from your budgeting that you will have about $7,000 in the chassis, the same in the engine and transmission, another $10,000 in the fiberglass body kit and another $10,000 in miscellaneous costs like interior and paint. What most people do is spread the cost out over the duration of the project.

For example, they buy the frame this month and later buy some suspension parts and slowly put the chassis together over time. They paint the finished chassis and move on to the engine. Maybe a year goes

by before they purchase the body and then they start prepping it for paint. They have a gorgeous chassis costing 15 grand or more and a newly painted body ready to go.

Then one day they invite their friends over to watch and help lower the body to the chassis. It is on this day that all the problems arise. First the firewall hits the engine and scuffs up the paint. Then the rear tires either stick out too far from fenders or rub on the inner fender wells. Then the brake and gas pedals don't line up. A few dozen choice words are said and eventually the blame goes to the kit manufacturer for providing

How will you want your front suspension to look? Much of decision is style rather than function. Will the suspension be visible? Early hot rod styles expose most of the front suspension.

a crummy kit. Some $25,000-plus is wasted and the project comes to a screeching halt—often for good.

Once again, this is the direct result of poor planning.

Buying the car piece by piece and building it over time can work, but it usually ends up being more expensive. The big lesson here: *Always perform a rough build before any painting or final assembly takes place.* You need the complete chassis, wheels, tires, engine, transmission and all the major body parts. This makes up almost ⅔ of the total price of the car, so buying all of this at once needs to be part of your plan. If this is impossible, then just keep in mind that you will be storing the parts for a while before any real work can begin, and this takes quite a bit of discipline. The rough build is the key to avoiding many headaches.

Welding choices

Michael Young, owner of Street Rods by Michael in Shelbyville, Tennessee, knows how to do things right. He has been building rods for more than 30 years.

So let's see how Young does it.

The basic frame is built first and Young starts with a frame rail kit from American Stamping. The

rail kit comes with the boxing plates and outer frame rails. Even though you can buy pre-manufactured cross members, Young prefers to build these himself using tubular steel. Over years he has found these cross members increase strength while leaving more room for exhaust components later on.

The frame rails are first placed in a jig and bolted in at the spreader bar hole locations. In order to get a clean, smooth look, the wrinkled areas caused by the stamping process are hammered out with a dolly. The inner frame rails are cut to fit and tack welded in place. He uses both MIG and TIG welding during the construction of his frames. Most people are using MIG welders now, mainly to reduce equipment costs. There are differing opinions on which of the two are the strongest welds, but both TIG and MIG welding can provide plenty of strength provided the proper technique is used.

In order for a MIG weld to work best, there needs to be about a 1/16-inch gap between the two welding surfaces. This allows the MIG welding wire to melt both surfaces properly. TIG welding proves useful in areas where there is no gap at all because it has the ability to melt deeper into the steel. In general, Young uses a MIG weld to complete the boxed frame rails and a TIG welder to assemble and install the tubular cross members.

The chassis starts with the frame rails. Michael Young prefers non-boxed or C-channel frame rails because they have a smooth, original appearance. He then welds the inner plate himself to get the finished, full-boxed frame rail. *(Street Rods by Michael)*

Young uses tubular steel in the center of the frame with removable transmission mounts. Location of exhaust, gearshift and brake pedals all need to be fitted and planned before paint. *(Street Rods by Michael)*

Suspension decisions

After the frame rails are centered in the jig and measurements are taken, the center cross member is installed. The rear cross member is nothing more than a tube or C-channel piece of steel and it, too, is welded into place. The front cross member is next, and it is at this point where we have some choices. The front cross member can change depending on what type of suspension will be used.

When hot rods were first built in the 1930s and '40s, there weren't too many suspension options. Most people focused on reducing weight and horsepower.

As better suspensions were introduced in new cars, rodders sought ways to incorporate these changes into the older cars. The easiest way to accomplish this was to replace the rear axle assembly and weld in the front cross member of a Mustang II or Pinto.

Most subframe replacements were done on post-1934 cars, however, and several problems were eventually discovered. First, when the original frame stubs were removed, all of the mounting locations for sheet metal and radiator support were lost. New ones had to be measured and drilled. Also, it was uncommon that wide tires would set correctly and this limited the choice of wheel rims rodders could

Straight axles are the more traditional look and can come in many styles. Split wishbone suspensions were the most common, but seem to be fading from use on lighter cars. This style is still common on heavier, '50s customs. *(Street Rods by Michael)*

use. Many of the steering boxes would mount close to, or interfere with, the headers. The brakes at the rear of the car were also affected because many of the donor brakes used the emergency brake to constantly reseat the rear pads. Many rodders left the emergency brake off because it can be difficult to set up and within a month were riding on the front pads only and wondering why.

Often, by the time one problem was solved, a new technology would come out and create a whole new set of problems. Fortunately, the technology has stabilized and the modifications are getting easier to handle. There are two broad styles of front suspension used today: the straight axle and the independent front suspension (IFS).

Straight axles

The straight axle is most commonly found on lighter cars from 1928-'34. A straight axle is essentially what was used on most of the older cars originally, but several common modifications have been made to improve performance. The split wishbone was perhaps the first. A split wishbone improves handling by moving the pivot point towards the outside of the frame and widening the stance.

Much of hot rodding and custom work is "looks,"

so you see many suspension innovations based on this. Hairpin and four-bar straight axle front ends are similar and evolved from this need. This technology uses slender tubular bars to secure the spindle in place. A hairpin uses three contact points to the frame and the four-bar uses four contacts. The four-bar setup is the most commonly used in early styled hot rods today. Four-bar suspension is almost always found on high boy or fenderless cars. It has a clean, elegant look to it.

The "pinched" front end is another type of straight axle found on fenderless cars. This is similar to a four-bar setup but is modified so the frame rails narrow and tuck in behind the radiator for a clean, sleek look. Pinched front ends also use coil overs in the front instead of transverse springs and shocks. A good source for straight axle components is Pete and Jake's Hot Rod Parts.

As previously noted, straight axles are normally used on lighter cars. They historically had poor handling and "bump steer" problems, but much of this has been eliminated. The steering problems were mainly caused by using a Mustang steering box, which had a long drag link that went from the pitman arm to the driver's side front spindle. The driver would feel the steering wheel jump or shake when the wheels hit a pothole or bump in the road.

An example of a hairpin front end. (*Street Rods by Michael*)

Hairpin and four-bar set ups are being used more and more in the lighter '30s era hot rods. They give a clean look to the front end. (*Street Rods by Michael*)

An example of a four-bar front end. (*Street Rods by Michael*)

Independent front suspension (IFS) is certainly the choice for builders seeking performance. The down side is that this suspension will add a few thousand dollars to the project.

This is called bump steer. Early rods had no front sway bars either, which didn't help.

The newer Chevrolet Vega steering box uses a cross steer system, which is shorter and pushes on the passenger side spindle instead of the driver's side. This steering keeps the suspension in line over bumps. This change has greatly improved bump steer on straight axle front ends. An experienced or professional hot rod and frame builder should be used in mounting both suspension and steering components. Steering components must have parallel symmetry to both the ground, the frame and themselves in order to eliminate bump steer and make the car safe to drive. This is somewhat complicated.

Some people have sought out independent front suspension as a means to eliminate bump steer.

Independent front suspension (IFS)

One of the first IFS donor cars was the Corvair. However, when the Mustang II was introduced in the '70s, it quickly became the new standard in IFS for custom cars, and now all independent front suspension is called Mustang II suspension, whether the parts come from the car or not. A wide variety of IFS kits are available today, the least expensive of

which uses the entire set of parts out of an original Mustang II and then replaces the worn parts like brake pads.

This solution does have some problems. Most of the drawbacks are the same that you get with grafting in the entire front frame portion of vehicles. IFS is larger than the original straight axle, so stock Mustang parts rub the inside fenders of many models. It is also not used much on fenderless cars like high boys for similar reasons. IFS is bulky and odd looking on high boys, but works fine if you are building a custom car with fenders.

Stock Mustang IFS parts also can lead to the same wider-than-original wheel track and limit your options in wheel selection. Several companies recognized this and began designing custom cross members with tubular 'A' arms to fit most any car and eliminate the stock problems. One of the leaders in this field is Fat Man Fabrications, which offers almost any IFS part you'll need.

IFS generally handles better than the straight axle, but it too, has a few drawbacks. To eliminate bump steer, you need to have all of the steering components lined up as precisely as the straight axle, so I also recommend you have a professional install your IFS components. Many a rodder has bought an IFS kit, installed it themselves and immediately

A finished frame without suspension parts installed.
(Street Rods by Michael)

Most cars had a leaf spring suspension in the rear up into the 1960s. Hot rodders opt to replace these springs with a higher performance option that incorporates coil overs.

noticed the same bump steer or worse.

Other than the bulky look on fenderless cars and the precision needed in the installation, IFS really has no other cons. It is actually preferred in all of the larger custom cars starting with '35 and up. Kits can be located to help you install IFS all the way up through the '60s, so it can be utilized on almost any custom project. Another advantage to independent front suspension is that it uses a rack steering box, which will give you a modern, precision feel to your handling on the road.

IFS is not cheap, though. A complete IFS kit with new parts runs between $2,000 and $2,500. Keep in mind that straight axles can be found in the $1,700 range, but you need to factor in the cost of a steering box and mount. When this is calculated, the IFS is only $100 more or so. They end up being really close.

Rear suspension choices

There are also choices to be made when it comes to the rear suspension. On almost any car we work on, we'll find leaf spring suspension used at the rear of the car. Most people still prefer leaf springs on the heavier 1935-and-later models simply because leaf springs handle the heavier weights well.

Remember that leaf springs attach to a moving shackle at the rear of the frame. This is done to allow the springs to flex on severe bumps. When leaf springs flex, they end up pushing the rear axle toward the rear of the car. With the exception of Indiana Jones, few of us have been able to see this happen. You need to figure in about an inch-and-a-half of play front and back. This could be significant if you are designing custom wheel wells. There needs

to be some space between the rear tire and the body of the car.

Leaf springs use traditional shocks and there are some limitations when it comes to adjusting for ride height. The primary reason why you don't see rear leaf springs often in 1934-and-earlier cars is that the springs end up being so short that you get a very stiff, uncomfortable ride.

Just like the four-bar setup on the front of these 1930s models, you typically see four-bar setups in the rear. Unlike the front end, however, there are several variations of four-bar setups in the rear.

The traditional four-bar runs the suspension rods parallel to the frame and uses a panhard bar to reduce lateral movement of the axle. Even with the use of a panhard bar, a slight side-to-side movement can be felt in more extreme cornering, which has prompted a modification of this setup to what is called a "triangular" four-bar setup. The top bars on this setup are angled in, which eliminates the need for a panhard bar. Once the panhard bar is removed from the equation, the exhaust is much easier to install.

For the triangular four-bar setup, the axle housing must be centered under the car. You would be surprised to find out how many cars have a drive shaft that runs at an angle under the car. Triangular four-bar setups must have a centered housing to work properly.

The ladder-bar setup is much like a hairpin setup for the rear. The bars are longer and reinforced, which helps torque the wheels down to the ground. A ladder bar is recommended if you are building a high-horsepower engine, but otherwise they are difficult to run exhaust through.

Another type of suspension is the "pro street"

Independent rear suspension is also available for high performance, but it has the same cost increases associated as IFS. Understanding the actual application before the build is critical to building a car in budget. Most people will not be racing their cars.

setup. Pro street cars are like any other hot rod except they use massive rear tires normally found on dragsters. Pro street bodies require extensive floor and wheel well modification to accommodate the extra-wide tires. This system is an extra-narrow four-bar setup and uses a diagonal link instead of the standard panhard bar to stabilize the rear end. All four use coil overs instead of the traditional spring and shock.

Coil overs are nice because they are easily adjustable for ride height. Just remember that they act as your shocks, too. Many rodders will try to use them to increase ride height to the point where the coil overs are almost fully extended. This means you are essentially riding on steel, so your first speed bump will probably knock your fillings loose.

Selecting a rear end

With the frame and suspension completed, we now need a rear end and differential. How do we know how to get a rear end and axles that are the correct width so our tires do not touch the body or stick out too far? This question needs to be asked on every street rod project.

It is at this point that a rough build of the car becomes necessary. We need to mount the body to the frame first. Line the body up so it is straight down the axis of the frame and centered from left to right. The body needs to be placed from front to back so the rear wheel housing is centered above the rear axle housing location.

The body, whether it is steel or fiberglass, will have several body-mount locations so the floor can

A good look at a triangular four-bar setup. Notice the top bars are angled to give lateral support. *(Street Rods by Michael)*

This setup shows a ladder bar suspension in the rear. Ladder bars are good for performance applications like drag racing, but are not as useful in everyday street cruising because of their low profile. *(Gibbon Fiberglass Reproductions)*

Coil overs act as both the shock and the spring. They are adjustable for proper ride height. Be careful not to overextend the adjustment on your coil overs or you will lose both your shock absorber and suspension effect. *(Gibbon Fiberglass Reproductions)*

When using fiberglass bodies, it is best to send the chassis to the body manufacturer. The manufacturer will usually be able to custom make a floor to match the chassis. This will help line up the doors properly. *(Gibbon Fiberglass Reproductions)*

It is important to check wheel placement before paint and bodywork. To do this, you will need the rims and tires that will be used in the final build. All too often, shop tires are used only to find that the actual tires are too big to fit in the wheel wells. *(Street Rods by Michael)*

The engine/transmission assembly is lowered to mark the locations for the engine mounts. The engine should be placed about 1 inch forward of the firewall. This firewall had to be cut out to make room for the distributor. *(Street Rods by Michael)*

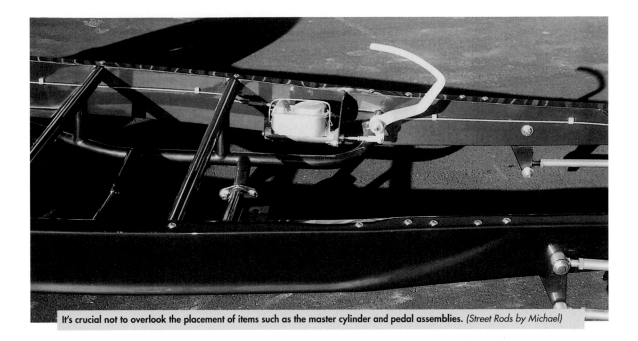

It's crucial not to overlook the placement of items such as the master cylinder and pedal assemblies. *(Street Rods by Michael)*

bolt to the frame. Cars from the late 1940s and later use rubber insulators between the frame and body. These can be located from Steele Rubber Co. Hot rodders usually use the stock frame in those years, so all you need to do is replace the rubber mounts and you are finished.

If you are using a fiberglass body, most kit manufacturers request that you send the chassis to them so they can custom manufacture the floor section to fit your chassis. This is necessary because every chassis is different and if you do not utilize this step, you may need some pretty radical shimming to get your doors to line up properly.

Most kits use a cloth-like mesh material as the body mount, often provided by the kit manufacturer. Some frames have tabs or ears that come off the frame for the mounts, and some frames have threaded holes right down into the frame. All mounts need to be checked at this point to see if they line up between the frame and floor.

Checking rear end fit

To get the proper rear-end width, mount the finished tires to the rims and roll them into their final location at the rear of the car. If you are not building a high boy, then you will need to mount the fenders as well. You can use jacks and jack stands to position the frame and body over the tires so they do not touch any portion of the body and they have sufficient ride clearance up and down. Custom steel-bodied cars with wider-than-stock tires usually need a floor and inner wheel well modification to allow for the larger tires. Your measurements and modifications could be made at this point.

The most important measurement you will need for the proper rear end width is the distance between the two mounting surfaces on the wheel rims. The mounting surface of the rim is the area that physically touches the disc rotor or drum. With the wheels in place, take a measurement across the width of the car from the inside mounting surface of one wheel across to the other. You should be able to contact any rear end shop at this point and give them this measurement. They will be able to provide you the proper rear end with axles included. When the rear end arrives, go ahead and install the rear end, coil overs, brakes and tires and double check that your measurements were indeed accurate.

Other details

The chassis will require a mock buildup. The engine, transmission, and radiator will need to be mounted for a test fit. You cannot skip this process. I think this step is necessary before engine and transmission mounts are put in place. There are times that the engine will not fit entirely in the engine compartment. In fact, most customs need a modified firewall in some way to accommodate a non-stock engine. This is the time to drill all the necessary holes around the frame for fender mounts, lines, exhaust and miscellaneous hardware.

The last critical measurements involve the gas and brake pedals. Every pedal kit mounts differently— some to the frame and others to the body itself. Either way a master cylinder or booster is almost always found on the frame just outside the pedal location.

All measurements and appropriate brackets

Once the engine and transmission have been mounted, the radiator and grille need to be mounted and checked for fit.
(Street Rods by Michael)

Most of the detail seen here is necessary for show cars, but not for cruising street rods. If your plan starts to go over budget, cut out the chrome on the chassis; it is the least appreciated.
(Street Rods by Michael)

need to be welded into place before any painting is done to the frame. Also, will you be using an electric fan to cool the radiator or a traditional engine-mounted one? Most rodders are having better luck with electric fans because they cool better in traffic and at lower speeds. It is a good idea to test mount the radiator and fan before painting as well.

Even when the chassis is essentially finished, you're probably still not at a point where you can paint the frame. Keep in mind that the body will be lowered to the frame for paint and bodywork so you are asking for all kinds of overspray problems if you finish the chassis at this stage. It is a good idea to get your chassis in a coat of epoxy primer for rust protection, however. Refer to the paint and body sections to learn more about proper metal preparation and the differences between paint and powder coating. If you go with powder coating, you should not prime any of the parts for any reason.

We will cover engines in the next chapter, but keep in mind that chassis assembly should be fun. This is where all the hard work pays off and you get to see the fruit of your labor. Remember that you cannot easily see the chassis once the car is completed, so the expense of chrome-plated parts and bolts is often not fully appreciated later on. Chrome is necessary on show cars, but this would be the first place to cut if it looks like you are going over budget.

Chapter 5

Engines

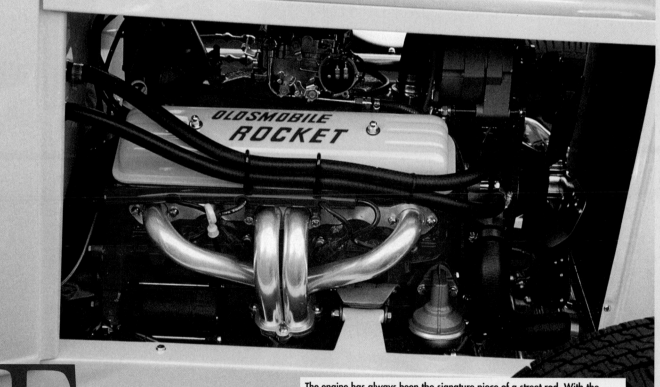

The engine has always been the signature piece of a street rod. With the right game plan, you can come up with an engine that looks as good as it runs without ruining your budget.

ENGINES ARE THE HEART AND SOUL of any hot rod. They give the car that hot rod sound and feel. Yes they are important, but they can definitely destroy your budget! A few common and deadly phrases come to mind: "If I just spend $150 more, I can get the same thing in chrome," or "The bigger the engine, the better," or "The next size short block up is only $1,400 more." Any of these thoughts can lead to the demise of the entire project.

Follow your plan strictly. Too often you'll see a $4,500 engine balloon into a 12-grand nightmare. Losing control of your plan starts with those little $150 compromises.

With that said, where do you start? Sometimes the decision is made for you. For example, big blocks just don't fit most of the smaller hot rods. Most of the massive engines you see at shows are never used for their intended racing application. Those expensive engines are there just for looks. If you have that sort of budget, fine. If not, you will need to exercise discipline.

Ultimately the application is key. Are we street cruising or racing? Do we want a nostalgic look? Eight-hundred-hp engines aren't needed or even

What do you really need? This 600-plus-horsepower engine is overkill for most applications. This engine adds $10,000 to the cost of the project for nothing more than bragging rights.

This engine will run you about $20,000. Will you actually be racing your car? If so, you may need this much performance.

useful in street cruising applications. The fact is that most people involved in hot rodding are street cruising. That puts them around 300 hp in a Chevy 327/350 or Ford 302/351. If you want nostalgia, then you will be rebuilding an original engine, or a flathead V-8. Of course, there are many other choices, and an entire book could be filled just on this subject alone.

The next question is whether you will buy a crate motor or build one yourself. "Crate" is the term for a new motor straight from the factory. This is fairly simple. The motor is new and has a factory guarantee. You assemble it into a long block, paint it, and install it. The other choice is to rebuild one yourself. Ideally, you save money building your own, and there are countless books on how to rebuild engines. However, I fear these books do more harm than good. If you are not experienced at rebuilding, or do not have access to the proper equipment, you run the risk of early engine failure. Of course, there is a chance the engine won't run at all. The inevitable mistakes caused by the learning process will only cost you more money in the long run.

I suggest a combination between the two. Crate motors are great for many applications and are the less-expensive option in most cases. So on a tight budget, crate motors are the way to go. My

An overview of this shop shows how much is involved in engine rebuilding. A full-service facility with countless large, expensive tools is needed to do the job right. *(Grooms Engines)*

only concern revolves around quality. There is only so much quality you can get from anything mass-produced. Slightly inferior parts will be used so long as they fall into tolerances. Having one built for you allows for more control over the process, and using a professional rebuilding shop eliminates the mistakes made from inexperience.

There are many engine rebuilding shops across the country. Chances are if they have been in business for more than 10 years, they are reputable. I suggest using one of the larger shops. The larger the shop, the higher the probability that they will have all the machining tools in house, and hence a greater control over quality. One such shop is Grooms Engines in Nashville, Tennessee.

Grooms got its start in the automotive high-performance field. It has 35 years of experience in building engines and has all the equipment it needs in-house.

Block

The process starts with the core. When a long block comes in, it has to be disassembled and inspected for potential problems. Often, pieces of former freeze plugs are found deep inside the water

After the engine has been torn down, the block is baked for 6 hours. This process turns years of grime into a flaky powder.

Blocks and heads are magnafluxed. This process finds any hairline cracks that can be missed by the human eye. *(Grooms Engines)*

A closeup of what a crack will looks like after it has been magnafluxed. *(Grooms Engines)*

After the block has been baked, it is blasted with steel beads to remove remaining grime and rust. *(Grooms Engines)*

A massive tumbler is used to work out any leftover beads or debris. *(Grooms Engines)*

galleys. If not removed, these parts will obstruct the flow of coolant and damage the engine. The blocks then have to be cleaned.

First, the parts are baked in an oven for 6 hours. The years of oil and grime turn into a crispy, powdered residue. The blocks are then put into a steel bead blasting cabinet and thoroughly cleaned. Small debris and leftover beads are removed with a large tumbler. Blocks and heads are tumbled repeatedly until the contaminants work themselves free. Once cleaned, the parts are sprayed with a chemical rust inhibitor.

The blocks are then magnafluxed (sometimes spelled magnifluxed). The technician sprinkles metallic powder over the block and applies a magnetic field. Should a hairline crack be present, the powder will form up around it. This crack is marked and a decision is made as to whether the crack can be repaired. Often, cracks can be repaired without compromising performance or reliability. When complete, the repair cannot be detected with the human eye.

The block is then sent to the boring machine. A block can be bored in a variety of ways. Most tools bolt onto the top of the block, also called the deck, and bore down into the block. They bore the cylinders in relation to the deck, but the cylinders travel in relation to the crankshaft. The machine Grooms uses aligns itself to the crank and then bores.

Most boring tools attach to the top of the deck. Grooms uses a special machine that aligns itself to the crank shaft so the cylinders line up as perfectly as possible. *(Grooms Engines)*

The difference may be slight, but every detail like this adds to engine life. Should a sleeve be needed, this machine bores a lip into the bottom of the cylinder wall to keep the sleeve in place.

With the cylinders honed, the block is then sent to a machine that surfaces the deck. It spins surfacing stones over the deck, taking any high or uneven metal off. This tool gives the heads a nice, level surface to bolt up to. Although this is standard, there is an additional step offered here. At this time, you could ask for square decking. A squared deck is cut so that every cylinder is equally distanced to the head. This is a very fine point and is only necessary for extreme engines operating in the 500-hp range or higher.

Most people think that honing an engine doesn't require much effort. If you have ever rebuilt your brakes, you probably used a small attachment to hone out the brake cylinders. Honing brake cylinders is fairly simple, however, honing engine blocks is a little more involved.

First, the block is put into a lathe-like tool that hones all of the main housing in one step. This ensures that the crank will turn true with no irregularities. Then the cylinders themselves are honed. Grooms uses water as a lubricant instead of oil because water controls heat better. The honing tool can bring the cylinders within .0002 of an inch to spec. The human hair is only around .003 of an

The cylinder boring machine in action. *(Grooms Engines)*

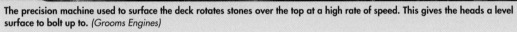

The precision machine used to surface the deck rotates stones over the top at a high rate of speed. This gives the heads a level surface to bolt up to. *(Grooms Engines)*

This unique tool is boring the main in its entirety so all of the surfaces are in line. *(Grooms Engines)*

After the cylinders are bored, they must be honed. The honing smoothes the surface and brings the tolerances within .0002 of an inch. *(Grooms Engines)*

Notice the difference in appearance between the bored cylinders and those that have been honed. Grooms uses a cross-hatching technique that improves oil circulation. *(Grooms Engines)*

Some of the final touches on the block are new cam rings and brass freeze plugs. Freeze plugs are in constant contact with water. Brass plugs are better than steel because they don't rust. *(Grooms Engines)*

Gaping holes? Steel freeze plugs rust like this. If you use brass, you won't have to worry about rust. *(Grooms Engines)*

Crankshafts should always be precision balanced. This eliminates vibration in the engine and throughout the car.

inch thick, so this equipment is amazingly precise. The honing technique used here offers one more benefit. It applies a crosshatch to the cylinder walls. This crossed etching helps pull oil up into the entire cylinder wall, which increases engine life. The cylinders are brush honed and cleaned.

Not enough emphasis can be put on cleaning. Honing stones leave grit, and this is what causes most bearing failure in new engines. If you decide to rebuild an engine yourself, you must clean the cylinders several times.

Engine components

With the block ready for assembly, we'll look at some of the component parts. Crankshafts can crack just like anything else, so Grooms utilizes an interesting technique for detecting cracks. If you tap the crankshaft to the floor, a good part will ring like a deep bell. Cracked parts will give a dull thud sound instead. Cranks are balanced and then sent to a machine that smoothes the bearing surfaces. Both crankshafts and camshafts are worked with a series of grinding stones until smooth. These surfaces are still not smooth enough at this point so they are polished. The micropolishing machine uses a finely gritted tape to work over the journals in stages until they

are smoother than glass. During these last polishing steps, a fine crosshatch is put on the bearing surfaces to improve lubrication.

Another example of quality control can be seen in the way this company handles rods. Even though a rod will look straight, it is often slightly twisted. Each rod is checked for this problem and corrected. This procedure relies as much on the skill of the individual operator as it does the equipment. Each rod has to be hand twisted back into shape.

The cylinder heads go through a similar process to the blocks. They are first cleaned and magnafluxed. Like the engine blocks, some cracked heads can be repaired. The heads are then decked and "ported." Ported describe the process of smoothing out the casting defects in the ports. The valve seats are then given a three-angled cut. This series of angled cuts improves airflow around the valve edges and allows the fuel mixture to disperse better inside the cylinder chamber. Both the porting and cut valve seats improve horsepower.

If a cylinder fires too early, the engine is experiencing detonation. It is caused by hot spots in the fuel chamber or when the compression ratio is higher than what the fuel is designed for. Diesel engines are essentially detonating all the time. In

A massive lathe is used to hone the crank journals smooth. Each of the bearing journals is a different length away from the centerline of the crank. This means that the machine must compensate for the wobble of the crankshaft as it turns in the lathe. *(Grooms Engines)*

A small amount of metal is being removed from this crankshaft journal to true the surface. *(Grooms Engines)*

One trick used to improve oil flow to the bearings is to slightly enlarge the oil hole at each journal. *(Grooms Engines)*

Several fine grades of polishing tape are used to work the journal surfaces down to a glass-like finish. *(Grooms Engines)*

Another look at a crankshaft being polished. *(Grooms Engines)*

Rods are checked for straightness and hand torqued until they run true. *(Grooms Engines)*

This head has been cleaned and decked. It now lies true to the block. You may notice slight bumps inside the ports. These casting imperfections are removed through a process called porting. *(Grooms Engines)*

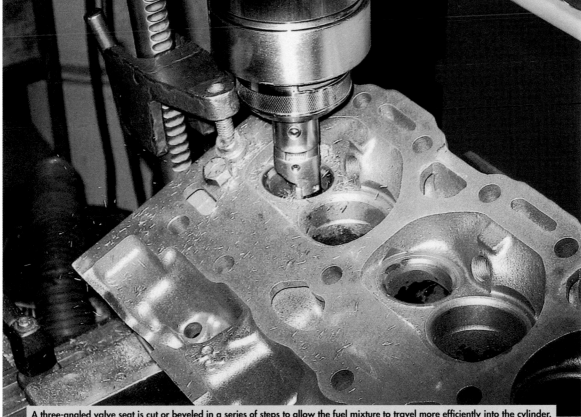

A three-angled valve seat is cut or beveled in a series of steps to allow the fuel mixture to travel more efficiently into the cylinder. *(Grooms Engines)*

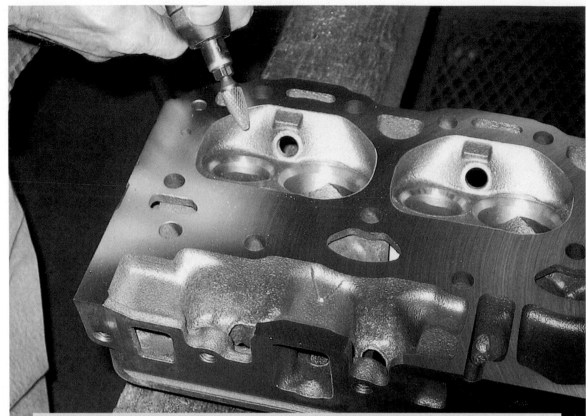

Most factory heads have a slight lip or flange that is created during the manufacturing process. These lips get hot and can cause your engine to misfire. They can be removed easily when your engine is being rebuilt. *(Grooms Engines)*

When a new engine first fires, there isn't any oil on any of the surfaces. To prevent damage, most engine builders use white lithium grease to coat and protect the bearings until oil has been pumped through all the gallies. *(Grooms Engines)*

The more chrome you use, the more you will pay. This engine runs close to $10,000. There is a wide assortment of engine pulleys available for Chevy motors.

gasoline engines, detonation damages the engine and robs it of power.

Often, factory heads have a slight lip or flange where the head and the cylinder meet. This is normal, but these flanges create hot spots that can cause detonation. Grooms removes all of these casting flanges. These little details add up and are the reason why I recommend a high-quality rebuild over a crate motor.

The engine is assembled and run through a series of tests to assure quality. On a bench, the engine is tested for oil pressure, oil flow, compression, and leaks. Possible leaks are found using a special dye that glows under fluorescent light. Should a leak be present, it can be addressed before sending the engine to the customer. Eastwood Company offers a dye similar to this if you are checking for any kind of fluid leaks at home. The engine is also tested on

an amp meter. The amp meter is attached to the crankshaft and lets the manufacturer know if the engine has too little or too much compression in the cylinders.

Most engines can be shipped out within two days. Each engine has a slightly different cost, but Grooms can be contacted for a free quote during your planning phase. If your cost for the motor is $4,000, you will still need to buy many more parts, like the starter, alternator, power steering pump, air conditioning compressor, water pump, distributor, pulleys and wiring harness. You are looking at a $6,000 expense total. The only way to cut back on this is to go back to our hot rodding roots and sort through salvage yards for used parts.

On the other extreme, let's discuss some of the higher-priced options and see what we can get for our money. As we go up in price, we are gaining

The engine needs to be in place, relative to the rest of the car, to determine where the engine mounts should be located. This builder is supporting the engine from above with a ceiling hoist. A common engine hoist can also be used for this step. The engine, transmission, radiator core support and inner fender wells will all need to be mounted before any painting should be done.
(Street Rods by Michael)

horsepower and chrome. A common engine in the $15,000 range would have extras like these:

502 big block with aluminum heads	$6,955
Block castings ground smooth and painted	$1,000
Aluminum heads polished	$400
Chrome tune port injection, wire harness and sensors	$3,895
Chrome alternator and A/C brackets	$295
Coated headers	$425
Chrome pulleys	$700
Chrome power steering pump and reservoir	$430
Chrome A/C compressor	$425
Chrome water pump	$105
Chrome alternator	$155
Chrome valve covers	$250
Performance cam	$185
Total:	**$15,220**

As you can see, the dollars pile up fast. Set a budget and stick to it. There are some very deep pockets in this hobby and you're not going to have bragging rights over every car you see.

Getting the right fit

Just about any part that bolts to the chassis should be test mounted before the chassis is painted. The biggest part, of course, is your engine and there are two important aspects of engine mounting. First, the engine must be far enough back so there is enough room for the radiator and cooling fans. However, the engine can't be so far back that it hits the firewall. Second, the engine must be at the proper angle. This is not as important for fuel-injected cars as it is carbureted ones. For carburetors to work properly, they need to be level or parallel to the ground. This means that all of the final suspension, wheels, and tires should be on the car to determine the vehicle's final rake or angle. The larger the rear tires are, the more rake it will have. Even though fuel-injected engines will run at an angle, they just look funny tilted forward. When you open the hood and display your engine compartment, people will expect everything to be level and orderly.

To find the right front-to-back location, install the distributor on the engine first. Then, using an engine hoist, lower the engine/transmission

One concern with engines is space. Will the engine fit under the hood? The engine should be purchased and test fitted before the bodywork phase. Large blocks just won't work in every application.

assembly to the chassis and slide the engine back so the distributor rests about 1 inch from the firewall. This is the ideal location for the engine. Obviously, the body needs to be mounted to the chassis. Therefore, the ideal time to do this is when you are performing an overall build of the car. This initial build is necessary to understand how the parts fit together. (This is discussed more in the fiberglass chapter.) Tack weld the engine mounts into place.

The engine is leveled by moving the engine or transmission mounts up or down. After the motor is in place and with the weight of the engine resting on the engine mounts, place a level on top of the block and tilt the transmission either up or down until the assembly is level. If there is not enough room to make all of the adjustment in the transmission mount, the engine mount can be cut loose and modified to compensate. I recommend bolting the transmission mount to a cross member as opposed to welding. If you need to remove the engine later on, a bolt-on mount will greatly ease engine removal.

At this time, you would finish your mock buildup of the car. It is important to assemble the engine compartment and mount the hood. Any miscellaneous mounting locations should be identified through this process. Usually you will need

to drill and tap additional mounting locations to the frame. It is nice to get all of this behind you before you paint or powder coat the frame. The purpose of mounting the hood is to make sure the engine does not contact the inside of the hood when it is closed. If it does, the hood will need to be modified or a smaller air cleaner will be needed.

After the mock buildup is completed, the parts can be disassembled and prepped for paint. The chapter on paint can walk you through the process. I recommend that a professional paint your body as the skill takes a long time to acquire. However, small chassis parts are a great training avenue if you want to learn how to paint.

Most people are powder coating chassis components these days. Powder coating offers a similar finish to paint with a lot fewer toxic emissions. Eastwood Company offers a small powder coating kit that can be used for any part small enough to put in your oven.

Powder coating is great, but I still prefer paint. It could be that I'm old fashioned, but more likely the reason is that I already have all of the equipment. The price of paint equipment can add up, and if you see yourself painting only one car, you are better off sending your parts out.

Chapter 6

Brakes

In most vehicles, brake components are not visible, so there is no reason to pay extra for chrome. The opposite is true in this case.

My FIRST SHOP WAS RUN OUT OF AN AIRPLANE HANGER and it never ceased to amaze me that people who knew little about airplanes and who never worked on one before would build kit airplanes and attempt to fly them. At least if you make a mistake with your car engine, you can usually pull over and call a tow truck. You don't have that luxury in the air and I feel brakes are just as serious.

For those who have never built a car before, you should enlist the help of a professional when it comes to most brake work. This is not the place to learn from your mistakes. With custom brakes, everyone is doing something different. In other words, there is more than one way to skin a cat. This chapter hopefully gives you the overall picture, but others may have a slightly different view. You'll have to roll with the information as it is presented and weigh all the opinions.

It's important to treat the brakes as a singular system and not just a grouping of parts. This means that the cylinder, calipers, lines and master cylinder match each other. A common mistake that rodders make is buying mismatched parts. Consult your brake parts supplier or builder and make sure you

Typical Disc/Disc Set Up

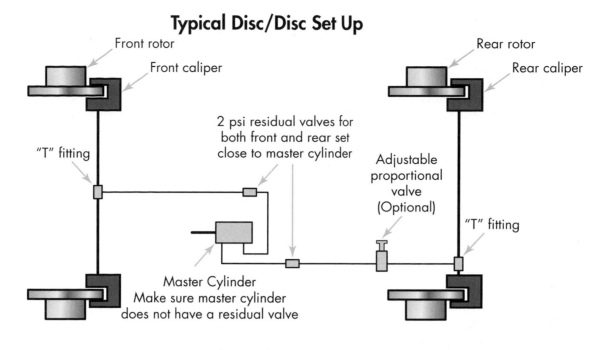

Typical Disc/Drum Set Up

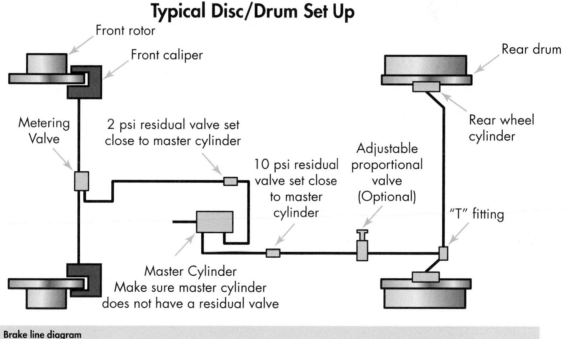

Brake line diagram

are buying parts that work together.

The most frequent complaint I hear about brakes in custom cars is a hard brake pedal. This is when you have to press down hard on the pedal to get the vehicle to stop. The extreme case would be the feeling that you have to "stand" on the brakes to get them to engage. Another problem happens when you apply the brakes and your rear tires lock up quickly. Of course, the worst problem would be a complete brake failure, when you press the pedal to the floor and nothing happens. There are usually simple explanations for these various problems.

In order to build a brake system properly, it helps to first understand what all the individual parts do. The design of your braking system will change radically if you intend to race the car, but the vast majority of custom cars are built for cruising. This chapter will focus on conventional braking systems used in street rods and passenger cars.

Types of brakes

There are essentially two styles of brakes: disc and drum. The most common factory setup today

This rotor is vented and has extra holes for improved cooling. *(Street Rods by Michael)*

uses both. You see discs in the front and drums in the back. If you remember back to your bicycle days, if you pressed the back brake only, you came to a slow stop. If you pressed the front only, you could flip over the handlebars. The best idea was to learn how to use both. Well, automotive brakes are similar in some ways.

The front brakes do most of the work. This is because the weight of the vehicle shifts to the front during the stop. To test this, watch the front end of your everyday driver dip down the next time you have to brake hard in traffic. If you were to pick up a disc, you would have your thumb on one side and your fingers on the other. You pick the disc up by squeezing it so that it doesn't slip out of your hand. This is how disc brakes work. The metal disc is called a rotor and your hand is the caliper. The caliper holds a brake pad on either side of the rotor and uses hydraulic pressure to squeeze the rotor to a stop. If this happens while the car is still moving, your tires lock up and you lose control. Anti-lock brake systems (ABS) have sensors that detect this and use a computer to pulse the calipers on and off so they don't lock up. Drum brakes use pads that press outward on the inside of a metal drum. The friction

slows the movement of the drum and brings the car to a stop.

If you are using drum-style brakes at the rear of the car, the brakes generally come with the donor rear end. So if you select a 1967-'74 Camaro rear end, then you will use those same drum brakes. Companies like Engineered Components Inc. can provide the rebuild kits for most rear ends you come across. If you are using a chassis builder, ask them which rear end and braking system will work best for your frame.

Early hot rods typically use a Ford 8- or 9-inch rear end. Cars up through the 1950s and '60s most likely will use the stock rear end and drum brakes and use a kit to replace the worn parts. Disc brakes are almost always used on the front and sometimes on the rear as well. None of the older cars had disc brakes, so a completely new kit will be needed to accomplish this. Most of the front end suppliers mentioned previously also supply the appropriate brakes.

Rotors

There are two basic types of discs or rotors. Solid

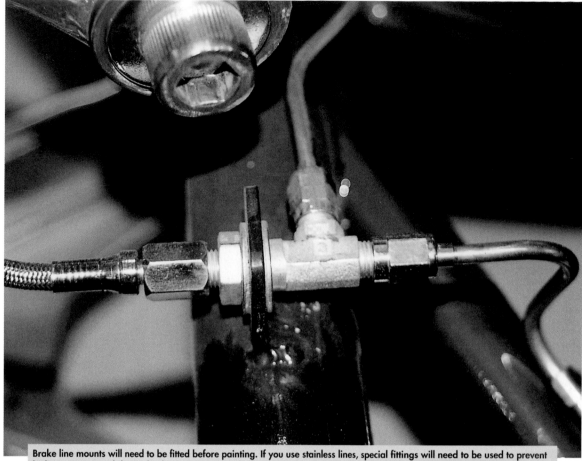

Brake line mounts will need to be fitted before painting. If you use stainless lines, special fittings will need to be used to prevent leakage. *(Street Rods by Michael)*

rotors are commonly used on early hot rods and are the least expensive. A vented rotor is hollow with small vents in the center to help cool the rotor down during heavy braking. Both styles can have extra holes drilled throughout the surface of the rotor to assist with cooling as well. Solid rotors will not cool as well as vented ones, so they are not recommended for cars weighing more than 2,800 lbs.

Most pre-1933 hot rods are close to 2,500 lbs. and are kind of on the borderline for use with solid rotors. When in doubt, use vented rotors, as they do not cost much more. Cars past '35 are almost always more than 2,800 lbs., so you should consider vented rotors on just about every car past that. Remember that the larger the diameter of your rotors or drums, the less frequently the pad will be touching any one spot, which helps reduce heat.

Calipers

There are two types of calipers available: floating and non-floating. Floating calipers are the most common and are found on most OEM brakes. This caliper has one hydraulic piston that operates the pads on either side of the rotor. They are affordable and

have several advantages. Should your rotor have a slight depression or imperfection on the surface, the caliper will ride over the area freely much like the arm of an old record player. Floating calipers are also easier to bleed and maintain. They are more likely to flex, so most manufacturers make them out of iron or steel.

Most racing applications use a non-floating caliper, which has a piston on either side of the rotor. They are less likely to flex so the lighter, stiffer, heat-resistant metals can be used. They are more difficult to use and maintain.

Brake lines

Brake lines can be another source of total brake failure. Brake lines are either made out of stainless or milled steel. Stainless is mainly used for looks as it maintains its silver finish and doesn't oxidize; however, it is much more difficult to install. Normal steel brake lines require a standard flaring tool that puts a double flare at a 45-degree angle. This is what normal brake fittings use and if flared properly, they will not leak. Stainless steel is much harder, so if you try to use standard brake line tools, you will either

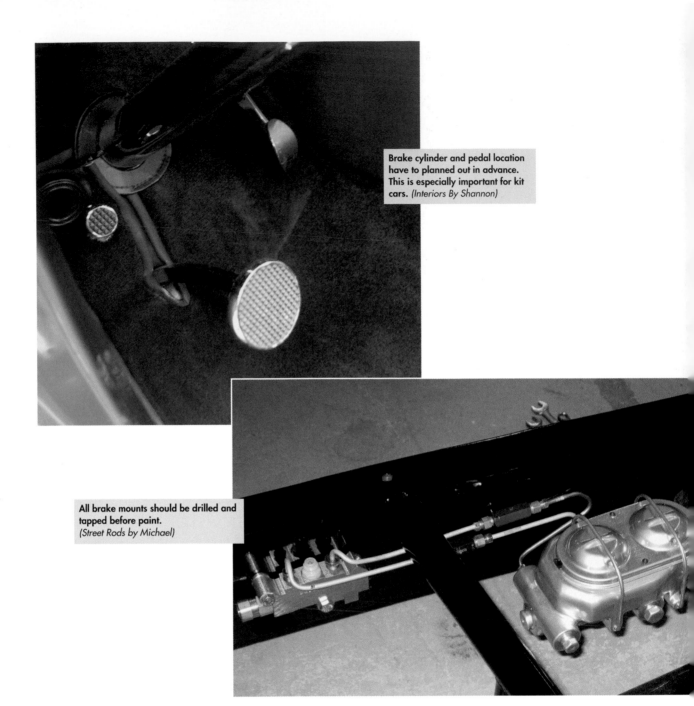

Brake cylinder and pedal location have to planned out in advance. This is especially important for kit cars. (Interiors By Shannon)

All brake mounts should be drilled and tapped before paint. (Street Rods by Michael)

split the end of the brake line or break the tool. Stainless is also much more difficult to bend.

If you choose stainless, you will need to use A/N (Army/Navy) fittings to prevent leaks. A/N fittings use a single flare at a 37-degree angle. There are special A/N fitting tools available for this. If you mix these two fittings up, your system will leak or fail. Most states also require a double flair on all brake lines, so if your brakes fail because of the wrong flair, you could find yourself personally liable for an accident. Most people use stainless only in show car applications.

The most common brake line diameter used is 3/16 inch, but there are exceptions. Some calipers or cylinders require more volume and may need larger, 1/4-inch lines. This is why it is important to view brakes as a complete system. Some parts require special items to work properly.

One word of caution: Never use compression fittings on your brake lines. They can blow out under high pressure, which will result in a total brake failure.

Valves

A series of valves are located in the brake lines. They often go unnoticed because so many OEM applications build the valves into the master or wheel

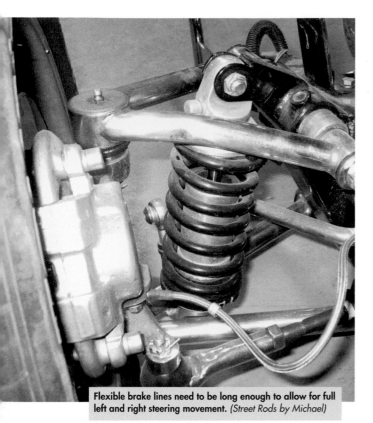

Flexible brake lines need to be long enough to allow for full left and right steering movement. *(Street Rods by Michael)*

Disc brakes are available for almost any make or model. *(Street Rods by Michael)*

cylinders. Ask your brake supplier if these valves are built in. Many of the valves have more than one name, but if you describe the function, you should be able to communicate with the brake supplier what your needs are.

The first valve is a metering or hold-off valve. This is used in a disc/drum setup only and makes sure that the rear brakes engage just slightly before or at the same time as the front discs. This valve is not usually used on disc/disc setups.

Another valve is a proportional valve. It is used in both disc/drum and disc/disc setups, but not typically used with hold-off valves. Proportional valves allow the rear brakes to come on first, but also create a slight pressure delay to the rear brakes so they don't come on at full force as soon as the pedal is applied. In other words, you want the rear brakes to come on first so the car doesn't swap ends, but you don't want them to come on so strong that the rear locks up.

Proportional valves are often confused with adjustable proportional valves, which work much like a water faucet. Adjustable valves allow you to restrict the flow of brake fluid to a set of brakes. Most street rodders use them to reduce the strength of the rear brakes, which is not what they were designed to do. Originally, adjustable proportional valves were used in racing. Racers use two of these valves to control fluid moving right and left and then run the valve up

into the passenger compartment. This allows them to reduce or shut off the brakes of one whole side of the car, which is very useful in oval track racing.

Pro street cars have very large rear tires that grab or lock up easier because of their larger surface area. Rodders who drove these types of cars began using proportional valves to cut off some of the fluid to the rear brakes to bring balance back to the system. After the valve started working well for the pro street crowd, many rodders put them in their systems. It is common to see these valves set to a zero or nonfunctioning setting, because they are just not needed in non-racing hot rod and custom cars.

The last type of valve is referred to as a residual valve. Residual valves are used to maintain pressure in the lines and are needed in two cases. On disc/drum setups, a 10 psi residual valve is needed for the rear drum brakes. The cup seals inside a drum wheel cylinder are designed to seal in one direction, so if 10 lbs. of pressure are not applied at all times, the seal will leak air into the lines every time you release the brake pedal. Keep in mind that many master cylinders designed for drum brakes already have a 10-lb. residual valve in place, so you may not need to add one. Ask your parts supplier which type you have.

Disc brakes do not need a residual valve unless the master cylinder is physically located below the brake calipers. A good rule of thumb to follow is

How to Calculate Pedal Ratio

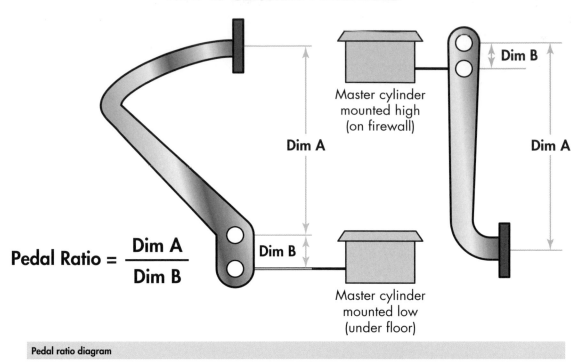

$$\text{Pedal Ratio} = \frac{\text{Dim A}}{\text{Dim B}}$$

Master cylinder mounted high (on firewall)

Master cylinder mounted low (under floor)

Pedal ratio diagram

that if the master cylinder is located on the firewall like most cars after 1934, the cylinder is higher than the calipers. If the master cylinder is located on the frame below the floor, then it is lower than the calipers so every time you release the brake pedal, brake fluid will have a tendency to run downhill back to the master cylinder. A 2 psi residual valve is needed to prevent this. One exception is in pro street cars where the rear end is elevated radically and ends up being higher than the master cylinder no matter what.

Just remember that if you are driving and you need to pump the brakes several times to build up pressure, there may be a problem with the residual valves, or you may need to add them to the system.

Pedal ratio

Ultimately, a hard brake pedal may be the result of a problem between the master cylinder and brake pedal. To better understand how they work together it helps to understand what pedal ratio is and how it interacts with the diameter of the master brake cylinder.

Pedal ratio is a measurement of how much leverage, and therefore force, will be applied to the master cylinder. The longer the lever that the brake pedal is attached to, the greater the force. So why aren't pedal arms 2 feet long? Well, they would stick way up into the passenger compartment, so there is a balance

between length and practicality. High pedal ratios usually mean that you have to lift your foot up in the air off of the gas to apply brakes, and that is not user friendly.

One of the reasons for hard brake pedal is that the pedal ratio is too low, meaning the length of the pedal arm is too short. Your pedal ratio should be a minimum of 5 to 1 and works well around 6 to 1. You can measure this by first taking the length from the end of the pedal arm (about the center of the pad) down to the pedal pivot point. Then divide that number by the length from the pivot point to the master cylinder contact point.

The diameter of the master brake cylinder is also important. You can calculate the total amount of pressure applied to the system by using this formula:

Let's look at an example. If you apply 75 lbs. of force to the pedal and your pedal ratio is 6 to 1, then your top number is 450. If you use a 1-inch diameter master brake cylinder then your bottom number would be 1 x 1 x .785, which is .785. So 450 divided by .785 equals 573 psi, or pounds of pressure, in the lines.

It is tempting to use a 1 1/8-inch master cylinder thinking more is better and if you push more fluid you will stop the car better, but using this formula you'll see that you actually reduce the amount of pressure to 453 psi. You do indeed displace more fluid, but the fluid is under less pressure. So why not use a smaller cylinder like a 7/8- or 3/4-inch master cylinder? Because you will have more pressure in the system and the pedal will be easier to push.

The problem with this is that the cylinder will displace less brake fluid than needed, so you'll push the pedal all the way to the floor and still not engage the brakes. The bottom line with brakes is that a 1-inch master cylinder is a good rule of thumb, but there are certain wheel cylinders or calipers that require larger or smaller master cylinders. Disc and drum brakes are easier to engage, so it may be a good idea to use a disc/drum setup on your first car or until you become more familiar with brake systems.

Disc/disc systems may stop the car better, but they are harder to engage and frequently require a brake booster to operate properly. Brake boosters operate off of the vacuum from the engine, and most hot rod engines don't create much vacuum due to the racing cams used.

So going back to that planning lesson: If you want to use a four-wheel disc setup, it's a good idea to let your engine builder know that you will need 16 to 18 inches of vacuum to run your brake booster.

Brake fade

One of the reasons for total brake failure is "brake fade." There are different kinds of brake fade and they are most commonly found during performance situations, like racing or negotiating long, steep grades. If you watch NASCAR racing you may have seen some of the spectacular undercarriage shots of the brakes getting so hot they literally glow red. This really doesn't happen in street cruising, so don't feel like you have to design a $10,000 brake system. Brake pad fade is caused when the pads get so hot the resins begin to liquify. The melted resin acts as a lubricant between the pads and rotors. Racers avoid this by using metallic or carbon pads and multiple calipers per wheel. Organic pads are generally recommended for those of us who are not racing.

Most modern cars have semi-metallic pads. Organic pads do wear out faster, but keep in mind that most street rods are not everyday drivers, so the pads aren't used as much. Organic pads grab the rotors better in normal conditions and require less pedal force to operate. The more metal flake that is in the pad, the more pedal force is required to operate them. Metallic or high-performance pads will only make a hard pedal worse.

Calipers can also cause another type of brake fade. If a caliper gets too hot, the brake fluid can boil and lose its hydraulic properties. This is called "fluid fade." "Deflection" is a term used to describe how calipers stress or flex under load. Metals like steel and cast iron flex the least, but they absorb and retain heat. Aluminum and magnesium will flex more, but dissipate heat much faster than steel. For everyday use, cast-iron is affordable and works fine, but exotic metal calipers are offered for racing applications.

One way to reduce fluid fade is to use different kinds of brake fluid. Dot 3 is the standard and works well for most applications. It has a few drawbacks, though. It boils at high temperatures, which means it can be bad for racing. It also absorbs or attracts water and the only solution for this is to replace it when it starts to look dark brown. Perhaps the most frustrating thing about Dot 3 is that it is an excellent paint stripper. If you get a leak, it will easily strip the paint off any surface it sits on.

Silicon or Dot 5 fluid is different. It resists water, doesn't boil, and doesn't attack paint. It seemed like a miracle when it came out, and in the 1980s and early '90s everybody was switching to the stuff. A bizarre incident happend while I was managing a paint shop. We, too, made the switch and really liked the Dot 5, until one day an employee spilled a quart of it on the floor in the back of the shop. We cleaned it up the best we could and didn't think much of it again. Shortly thereafter, we began having severe paint problems. We were getting fish eyes all over the place and couldn't get rid of them until I started to remember that silicon and paint don't mix. No one ever told me that silicon could go airborne like that, but it does. It was so difficult cleaning the silicon out of the shop that I banned anything that had silicon in it from that day forward. That means brake fluid, polishing compounds, lubricants, sealers, etc. Unless you race, Dot 3 should be just fine. Whichever you pick, do not mix the two as they are not compatible and the seals in the system will fail.

Brakes are definitely an area you don't want to overlook when mapping out your build. If you aren't sure how to proceed, seek out advice. By working with a professional to plan your first brake system, you should have brakes that are both easy to use and safe.

Chapter 6
Fiberglass Bodies

Most of the finishing parts do not come with a fiberglass kit. It's important to know what you're getting before you part with any money. The details are what will make or break your project. *(Gibbon Fiberglass Reproductions)*

SOME OF THE MOST BEAUTIFUL CARS around are fiberglass-bodied hot rods, but there are some things about them that can be surprising or disappointing to the newcomer. I think most people expect them to be as easy to put together as the plastic models we built as children, but they are not. In fact, most of the failed or abandoned hot rod projects start out as fiberglass kits.

When we hear "kit," we expect it to be 100 percent complete, and all we will have to do is open the crate, read the directions and start putting the thing together. Expectations seem to be that in a few weekends, you'll be driving your new kit car down the road. Very few manufacturers have a step-by-step guide on paper. When you buy a kit, what arrives are the basic body parts only. I've attended numerous car shows and sometimes give "how-to" lectures. I couldn't begin to count how many stories I've listened to over the years concerning failed kit projects and every owner seems to conclude that the kit manufacturer "ripped me off!" However, the real reason why these projects failed is poor planning and false expectations.

What's in a kit?

Fiberglass-bodied hot rods are kit cars, plain and simple. There are hundreds of kit car manufacturers

Fifteen years ago, fiberglass bodies were limited to 1932 Fords, but now a wide variety of models are produced. *(Interiors by Shannon)*

making everything from old Duesenbergs to futuristic space cars. There are dozens of hot rod body manufacturers and the prices of their kits vary significantly. Naturally, we look at the low-cost kits and say, "All 1932 Fords are equal, so why not go with the lowest bidder?" The simple answer is, we get what we pay for and all kits are not equal. The lowest-cost solution may work for the government when it builds bridges, but it rarely works for street rodders. You should expect that the kit will be a body and nothing more.

Most hot rods will have some 3,000 to 6,000 parts, and most body kits have just a few dozen. Don't expect neat little packages containing all the nuts and bolts you need for the entire car. Some manufacturers offer this as an option for a fair price, and I highly recommend it. Most kit car manufacturers do not build the chassis themselves, but the better ones have established relationships with chassis builders and also offer a semi-complete chassis as an option. The advantage in purchasing this option is that these contractors understand the little "quirks" of the kit, which is very helpful. They usually know where to put the body mounts and brake or gas pedals. You will save very little money trying to build the basic chassis yourself.

The electrical wiring harness can be another challenge. Always ask if the kit builder offers this as an option. If they don't, they should be able to point you to someone that has it. The better manufacturers offer all kinds of supplementary kits, like door handles, bezels, glass, gauges, etc. In other words,

there is the basic kit on one hand, and another kit that has all the parts you really need.

It is important to ask questions about the kit. The danger here is that a hot rod builder may have a budget for $7,000 and get excited to find out that the kit is only $5,000. After the purchase, they discover the kit requires another $15,000 in parts to complete. Understanding what is included before the purchase is crucial because most kits are nonrefundable so you are locked in as soon as the kit arrives. Looking for the hidden costs will reduce the risk for failure.

Formulate a priced checklist of all the parts that come with the kit as well as the "extras" needed for completion right down to the gaskets and washers. Sometimes the less-expensive kits have so few parts that they really are more expensive when you make an apples to apples comparison.

The less-expensive kits usually require extensive engineering as well. Common issues seem to revolve around the doors, trunk and hood. I've seen kits that provide a body and a pair of doors right out of the mold with no hardware at all. The novice gets one of these kits and then has to figure out how to mount the doors, where to drill the holes and how to make the door hinges from scratch. The better kit manufacturers will offer to deliver the kit with doors and other panels already mounted. This is the best option!

Find out if the manufacturer provides a turn-key option. This means that they build the entire car right down to the paint, chrome, interior, etc. A turn-key kit is essentially a brand new car, ready to

Pro street cars are more difficult to plan because the manufacturer of the body kit needs to see the finished wheels and rear suspension in place. The custom floor and wheel wells are made to match the size and position of the tires. A chassis builder familiar with fiberglass can help. *(Gibbon Fiberglass Reproductions)*

go. You just show up, they hand you the keys and you're gone! I recommend that you only do business with companies that offer turn-key solutions, not because you have to buy it this way, but you would be surprised how many fiberglass companies have never even built their own kit! Chances are, if they haven't built their kit, they will not be a helpful resource as you go. You need someone reliable to speak with if you get stuck during the build and need help.

Stick with a solid company

Gibbon, Downs, and Redneck are all reputable companies and are used by professional builders. Of course, there are other fine manufacturers, but there are many bad ones as well. I wish I could print a list of the ones to avoid, but I would probably spend the next 10 years in court. Bottom line: Don't purchase anything until you speak with other people who have built the same kit and feel comfortable recommending the company to others. I'll be using Gibbon Fiberglass Reproductions as the example.

As with hot rods themselves, fiberglass technology has been continuously refined over the years. One of the challenges in fiberglass is dealing with expansion and contraction in the material. Both steel and fiberglass expand and contract, but with fiberglass the movement can cause cracking in the body over time. With steel, only the paint will crack.

Opinions on how to best deal with this problem have changed over the years, but at one time it was thought that your fiberglass body would be stronger if it had few seams. For a while, bodies were made to be almost one-piece units. The problem with this concept is that there were no places for the body to expand and stress cracks eventually begin to show at the 90-degree corners of the body.

Gibbon builds the body as several mini body parts and bolts them together to form a singular car body, in much the same way original cars were assembled. You have a separate floor, firewall, roof, etc., and then assemble these so that the seams lie in natural expansion areas around the 90-degree locations of the body.

The fiberglass panels can be made in different ways. The most common is a hand-laid procedure where fiberglass mat is soaked in resin and laid in the mold in layers. If this is done properly, the fiberglass becomes strong and is usually 3/16 to a 1/4 inch thick.

The inside of the body panels are rarely gel-coated, so be sure to inspect these areas. Improperly laid fiberglass will have frosty white areas where air bubbles or dry fiberglass have accumulated. This fiberglass will be weak and crack easily. Gibbon uses a roller to press the fiberglass properly against the mold to work out the air bubbles and properly saturate all of the fibers.

One drawback to fiberglass is the lack of originality. Many identical car bodies are being produced so the only customization options occur with the paint and interior. (Gibbon Fibeglass Reproductions)

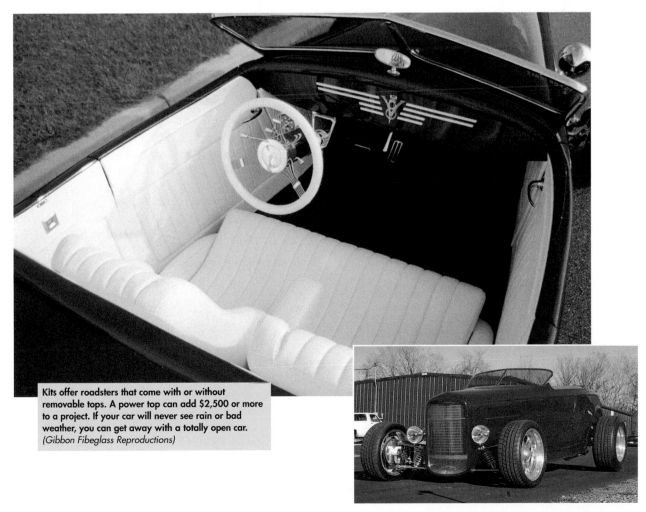

Kits offer roadsters that come with or without removable tops. A power top can add $2,500 or more to a project. If your car will never see rain or bad weather, you can get away with a totally open car. (Gibbon Fibeglass Reproductions)

This five-window fiberglass car has been test fitted onto the chassis and is ready for the bodywork to begin. It will eventually get fenders, running boards and other bodywork pieces. (Street Rods By Michael)

wood. Gibbon chooses mostly wood reinforcement, but it uses steel in the firewall to support the steering column and door hinges.

Gibbon also offers several key options. First, it will build your floor custom to your frame. This is important, because the company provides its kits standard with the doors and trunk lid mounted and adjusted. This service is already included in the price of the kit, so make sure that you compare apples to apples when you shop around.

What good is it to have the body all set up at the factory, only to have a hot rodder start over with the adjustments because the body doesn't match your frame when it arrives? And how can I ship the finished chassis over to the manufacturer if I need the body to finish the chassis? Well, you can't, but all they need is the frame, not the whole chassis.

After your kit arrives

When your kit arrives, inspect all of the parts and make sure that none of the fiberglass is damaged and that all of the parts are there. If this build project lasts a few years, it isn't fair to call the manufacturer two years after purchase and claim a part is missing. Lay the parts out and see how they fit together. Most manufacturers will include a manual stating their advice for the build. Read this manual thoroughly before any work begins.

Fiberglass doesn't cure with time, it cures with heat and it will cure to the highest temperature it is

Fiberglass bodies should have reinforcement inside the body as well. Some companies use steel, others wood. Gibbon uses both, depending on the need. Wood has some advantages in that the pores absorb the resin and bond with the fiberglass. It also is easy to tack upholstery or screw small fasteners to

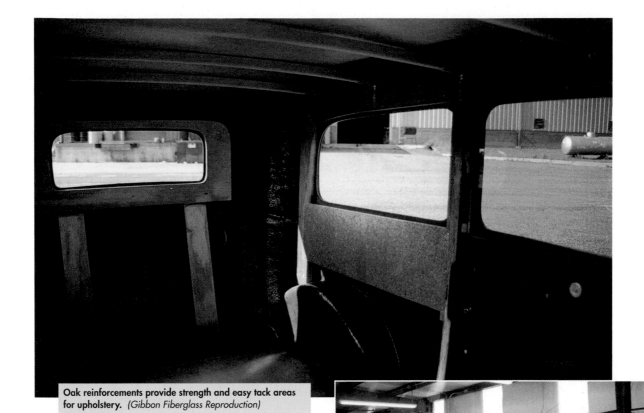

Oak reinforcements provide strength and easy tack areas for upholstery. *(Gibbon Fiberglass Reproduction)*

exposed to. Many rodders have found out the hard way that a car gets real hot out in the sun. I remember inspecting a car in west Texas one summer. It was the usual 107 degrees in the shade, and I made the mistake of leaning against the car. Immediately, I jumped back in pain. The "friend" I was with got a good chuckle out of it, but I had a first-degree burn in just that second's time. Judging on how quickly I got burned, I guess the car's surface was between 160 and 170 degrees. This was a light-colored car, too. The darker the color, the hotter the surface will get.

To test this more accurately, I rolled a red car I had recently painted outside to heat up. It was around 70 degrees and I wanted to cure the paint faster. After the car had been sitting for an hour, I put a thermometer against the paint and it read 155!

Most manufacturers cure the fiberglass up to 110 degrees, but that is not enough. As fiberglass cures, the surface gets slightly bumpy or orange peeled. A lot of builders don't understand this until the car is finished and is being shown for the first time. At the beginning of the show the car looks great, and by the time the show is over, the car's paint looks rough. This is because they were curing the fiberglass for the first time and it changed texture in the process. This will happen even if the fiberglass is many years old.

To avoid this, take all of your fiberglass parts and place them out in the sun on a hot day. This can

The bodywork process can be simple, or very involved and time consuming. The number of modifications the fiberglass will require depends on the quality of the kit.

When a fiberglass body kit arrives, it is important to lay out all the components and check to see if anything is missing. *(Gibbon Fiberglass Reproductions)*

Note the flashing lines near the firewall and above the windsheild. This manufacturer finishes these for customers, but not all companies do. *(Gibbon Fiberglass Reproductions)*

Fiberglass doesn't cure with time, it cures with heat and will cure to the highest temperature it is exposed to. When your fiberglass body arrives, be sure to set all the pieces out in the sun. *(Street Rods By Michael)*

blue on fiberglass cars due to this same heat and curing issue. After the curing process is complete, you can begin the rough build.

Cleaning up the body

Your next step is to perform the rough shaping and cutting of the fiberglass. If you remember your plastic model days, you had to clean up and trim down the seams of the model. This is because there was excess plastic where the part touched the mold. Fiberglass is no different. The seams where the mold bolts together will leave extra material on the body. These areas of excess material are called flashing lines.

Gibbon repairs these for you, but that is not the norm in the industry, so these lines will need to be addressed first on most kits. With an abrasive disc or dual-action sander, grind the seams so that ½ inch on either side of the flashing line has been ground back and about 1/16 to 1/8 of an inch deep. The exposed area should be blown clean with compressed air. Bodywork techniques are addressed later in this book, but once the seams are cleaned, apply a thin coat of body filler along all of the exposed fiberglass and sand flush once it has cured.

certainly affect the planning process if you live in a cool climate, and laying parts outside in winter won't accomplish much. It is important to bolt all of the parts to the body before the curing process because the parts form to the body some while curing. The surface should feel hot to the touch, but if you have doubts, purchase an inexpensive candy thermometer and take a reading. The surface needs to get to 150 degrees or more. Most manufacturers will also encourage you to avoid dark colors like black or navy

Special attention is being paid to the engine side panel on this car. Keeping things flush and smooth is the key to eventually obtaining a great paint job. (Gibbon Fiberglass Reproductions)

All of your first work is just a rough go-around, so I would feel comfortable using power tools to sand your filler in this stage and an 80- or 120-grit should work fine. All of the gel-coat over the entire vehicle needs to be lightly sanded with the same grit paper to break the surface up for proper primer adhesion.

The rough build

The rough build is really similar to that involving the chassis, but with a new emphasis. We need to mount the body to the frame and go through the process of mounting the body parts like fenders, hood, doors, etc. Many fiberglass manufacturers will ship the body to you with doors and trunk lid installed. If they do, do not remove these! Go ahead and go through the build process to finish the chassis with suspension, drive train and wheels as in Chapter 4. All of the parts must line up and mate flush to the body. Bolt everything in place, including the fenders and running boards.

One of the characteristics of fiberglass is you cannot tighten the fasteners as hard as you can with steel, and this may feel strange at first. We have been told most of our lives to tighten everything down as hard as possible, but if you do that on fiberglass, you will crack it. The cracking or crushed effect is called "starring." Kyle Bond at Gibbon Fiberglass recommends using nylon lock nuts to secure any

The builder of this car is doing a rough build of the interior. This step helps determine if the steering column and shift lever are in the right place. (Gibbon Fiberglass Reproductions)

fiberglass parts, such as fenders. The normal pressure needed to compress a split washer is enough to crack the gel coat, so Bond uses the same bolt, flat washers on both sides, no metal lock washers and nylock nuts instead. Less torque is needed with nylon lock nuts to secure the parts. You also want to distribute the force out over the largest area possible, so the larger the flat washer, the better.

There should be few, if any, holes on the firewall and floor. I guess it could be considered lazy for the manufacturer not to cut the holes themselves, but every kit car is different and every chassis has mounts in different places. All that would happen is they would cut a bunch of holes that wouldn't be used, so the industry makes the safe play and leaves it up to you.

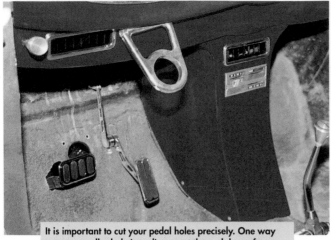

It is important to cut your pedal holes precisely. One way to get a smaller hole is to disconnect the pedal arm from the master cylinder and lower the arm down into the hole, rather than cutting a bigger hole. *(Interiors by Shannon)*

Fiberglass kits do not come with pre-cut holes in the firewall. This gives car builders more flexibility in selecting mounting locations. *(Gibbon Fiberglass Reproductions)*

You need a Dremel, cut-off wheel or Roto-Zip tool to make these cuts. The first cuts are always a little nerve-racking, so make them in low visibility-areas like the gas pedal or stick shift. The cool thing about fiberglass is that, even if you cut the hole in the wrong spot, you can glue the part back in place with resin. Fiberglass is very forgiving in that regard.

You usually need to cut holes for wiring, pedals, gearshift, windshield wipers, bumper brackets, headlights, taillights and turn signals. The best way to avoid a mistake is to start with a small hole and cut outward until you have the hole the way you like it. This method works well for the pedals and gearshift where some educated guessing is used to locate the proper spot. However, many of the holes are used to mount parts like the headlights. You can reduce errors by making a paper template of the headlight housing first and then trace the outline on the fiberglass before any cutting is done.

It's a good idea to make all of your cuts and mount all of the pieces before priming. The edges of all the parts like fenders, hood, trunk lid and doors need to be worked too. The fenders are perhaps the easiest. The excess fiberglass from the molding process needs to be trimmed off and all edges sanded smooth. The other parts are more involved. The body should already be bolted to the frame, then the doors, trunk lid and hood should be mounted and lined up.

Most manufacturers do not install the hood, so you will have to do this yourself. Hoods on the earliest Fords are fairly easy to do, but most other hoods have two major adjustments. First, the hinges need to be placed properly on the vertical plane. Usually this is obvious in the sense that with the hood closed, the hood rests above the cowl at the rear or strikes the cowl because the hinges are too low. It is difficult to get the hinges wrong on the horizontal plane. If you make a mistake this way, the hood will bind and not want to close.

Make the hinge-to-firewall adjustments first, and then check to see if the hood is lined up on the hinges properly. With the hood closed, it should be centered and have a uniform gap all along its perimeter. You may need to make adjustments on all the panels. After these adjustments, you may notice a few areas where the gap is not uniform. This is because the hood, doors and trunk lids have not been trued up to the body. The goal of the truing process is to have a uniform gap in all of the seams. The truing process is done after the surfaces have had their first coats of primer applied.

Using the techniques in the bodywork chapter, clean the surfaces to be primed and apply enough epoxy primer to cover the surface. This should take about two coats. Once it's dry, apply several coats of urethane high-build primer. With the panels closed, check the gap along the perimeter of all the panels. For example, if the gap at the top of the door is 1/16 inch and the bottom is 5/16 inch, then you know that the door has not been adjusted properly. However, if it is a uniform gap close to 3/16 inch all the way around with the exception of a few places, then the door edge needs to be trued. This is done by taking a sanding block and lightly filing the edges so the high spots or tight gaps are removed. You should be left with a smooth, uniform gap.

The body is now ready for the standard bodywork process. The bodywork should be done with the body still mounted to the frame. It's a good idea to remove the finished wheels and drive train to keep them clean. You may want to wrap the frame and suspension in plastic as well.

Sporting nostalgia, this owner ditched the side engine panels to expose a very clean flathead eight.

Trim and interiors

Most standard kits do not include any kind of trim. Trim can include taillight and headlight bezels, chrome window frames, door handles, latches, as well as any stainless or aluminum trim you might find on a stock car. Most hot rods lack a lot of these parts anyway, but you may want some chrome accents on the exterior to set off the paint. Most of the better kit manufacturers will offer an assortment of trim options.

Finally, it is difficult for a manufacturer to offer a custom interior kit, so the interior will have to be built from scratch. Most kits cost between $6,000 and $9,000. The wide assortment of options and accessories available can add an extra $5,000 or more.

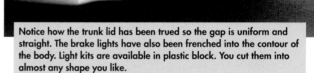

Notice how the trunk lid has been trued so the gap is uniform and straight. The brake lights have also been frenched into the contour of the body. Light kits are available in plastic block. You cut them into almost any shape you like.

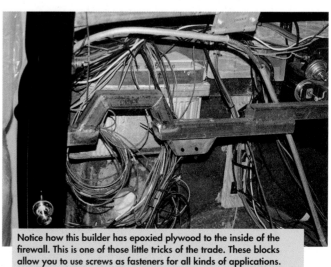

Notice how this builder has epoxied plywood to the inside of the firewall. This is one of those little tricks of the trade. These blocks allow you to use screws as fasteners for all kinds of applications. *(Gibbon Fiberglass Reproductions)*

Chapter 8

Metal Bodies

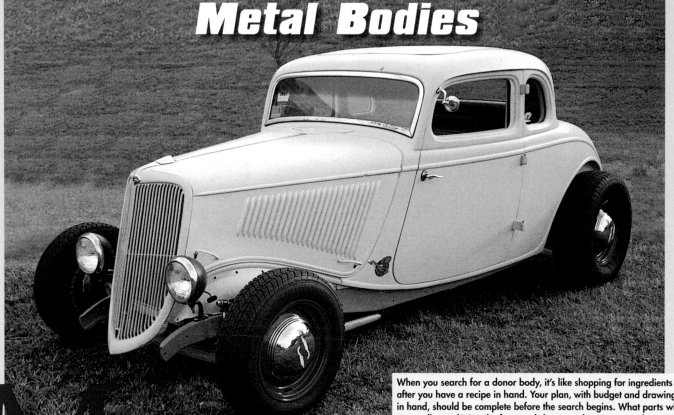

When you search for a donor body, it's like shopping for ingredients after you have a recipe in hand. Your plan, with budget and drawings in hand, should be complete before the search begins. What parts will you really need? Are the front-end sheet metal parts easy to locate? Will you need a set of nice stainless trim?

MORE EFFORT IS REQUIRED TO BUILD STEEL-BODIED custom cars than fiberglass ones. Your plan must address rust or collision damage as well as any custom modifications that will need to be done. Fiberglass bodies are new, so they won't be rusty or dented. They already have modifications like chopped roofs or hidden door handles. Steel bodies are a different matter.

Every potential donor car you look at will have some degree of rust. Small amounts of oxidation can be found on brand new cars, but most donor hot rod bodies are well over 60 years old and have been stored outside. The extent and location of the rust is the real issue. When you bought your last car, how

long did it take to get its first dent? Think about how long these cars have been around. The steel will have small dents—this isn't a big deal; but has the car ever been wrecked?

Understanding the costs involved in repairing and modifying metal before the donor body is even purchased is key to a good plan. As you shop around for the right body, make a tally of all the expenses needed to bring the metal to a "like new" status. It is very tempting when you find the right make and model advertised for $1,000 to say to yourself, "Hey, this is $9,000 less than a fiberglass kit, what a deal!" Add to this $1,500 to disassemble the body, $1,000 to strip the metal, $2,000 to repair rusted floor pans,

This is a typical car out in the field. It's difficult to inspect because of the grass and weeds around it, and the inside is filled with junk and spare parts. Take extra time to look these cars over before making a decision. If a car requires lots of replacement parts and rust repair, like this car, it's best to keep looking.

This floor pan is damaged in just the lower, flat portion that lies beneath the driver's feet. This is a common place for northern vehicles. Good donor vehicles are hard to find and you may be forced to settle with some problems.

$3,500 to chop the top, $500 to replace a damaged fender and so on. This tally of expense is the actual cost of the car.

So how do you know how much detail or finishing to ask for? The answer depends on the budget and whether you plan to show the car. Show cars are highly detailed, and can have $40,000 or more in metalwork expense. Most of the bill is wrapped up in subtle details. Judges have a trained eye for detail and can have discerning tastes. Cars now seem to be judged under a microscope and some custom car fans complain that judges at car shows have gotten too picky. The criticism may be

valid, and the winning show cars seem to have gotten out of reach for the average enthusiast.

As you seek out professionals for different stages of the project, take time to fully explain your intentions. Be careful with some of the terminology and jargon you hear, especially "show car." To say that you are building a show car to a professional may be interpreted far from the meaning you intend. The term "show car" to a professional often means that you have a budget of $100,000 or more and that the car will be shown in national competition. The shop owner will see the car as future advertising for the shop and assume that it needs to be a masterpiece.

This car has definitely been driven in the North. Salt is a car's worst enemy, and this car has little value even as a parts car. Look for donor bodies from the South and Southwest.

Show cars are rarely driven. Instead, they are usually hauled in a trailer from one place to the other. I know of too many stories where a novice customer dropped off a car with one intention and panicked when they saw the bill. The best way to avoid this is to simply tell the shop what your budget is and what you intend to spend. Withholding this information can only lead to misunderstandings later on. This process is not the same as when you shop for a new car.

Rust is a big factor

Rust is perhaps the most frustrating concern. It can be traced to areas that were poorly prepped during the paint process or areas the factory left unprotected. Rust progresses in stages starting with mild surface oxidation. As the damage continues, pits form and eventually turn into holes. These holes vary from pin size to more than a foot. One of the most troubling aspects of rust is that it can't always be seen at the time of purchase. Mild surface oxidation is difficult to detect under faded paint work. However, one thing to look for would be small bubbles forming within the paint itself. This lifting is usually caused by rust. As the problem progresses, the bubbles grow, and the rust begins to flake or scale. Interior trim, bumpers and moldings often conceal oxidized areas from view.

Rust is often found under factory undercoating and isn't seen until the car is stripped. Donor vehicles frequently find themselves in overgrown fields so the underside of the car can be difficult to inspect. Most owners are not going to allow you to remove portions of the car to give you full access, so a complete inspection may be impossible, but the more time you spend during the inspection the better. Bring a sheet of cardboard to lay on if you have to. Also bring a magnet, flashlight and telescoping mirror.

It's a given that vehicles driven in northern and coastal states are exposed to salt and are most likely poor choices for your project. When inspecting the body pay close attention to the wheel wells, floor, trunk and firewall. These areas are exposed to water the most often. Try to keep in mind that the greater the degree of oxidation, the more expensive the project will be. A point is eventually reached where the cost of the repair exceeds the value of the car, so it pays to be selective.

Avoid salvage projects

Small dents are not an issue, but collision damage repairs can be very expensive. Replacement panels are not always available like they are on modern cars, which means the body will have to be disassembled at the welds and custom patch panels made to replace damaged metal. With labor rates of $50 to $75 an hour, collision work can easily run $10,000 or more. My recommendation is to avoid a car that has been wrecked or has seriously deteriorated.

Metalwork considerations

Steel body modifications can also be costly propositions. Chopping, frenching and channeling are techniques that require skill to complete. If you do not feel comfortable with your metal working skill, you will need to enlist the help of a professional. All of these modifications have various levels of detail that can be added.

Chopping a top will typically run around $3,500. This sum will pay for the job to be done right by a professional, but the degree of detail and metal finishing will be very basic. There is an infinite number of extra details that can be added to a car body. These details are often subtle, but can be time consuming. For example, windows can be set at different angles, flat glass can be changed to curved, door pillar posts can change shape or angle, etc. All of these details add to and help define the overall theme of the car.

The degree that metalwork can be finished out is also variable. When custom metalwork began, both tools and techniques were limited. Most panels were brazed or welded in place in such a way that the panels warped. Modern polyester body fillers were not available, so large quantities of lead were used to smooth the shape of the car out and cover up seams. This is where the term "lead sled" comes from.

Today, metal work is much more refined. TIG welders use a foot pedal to adjust the heat so the welder only has to apply the minimum needed to melt the rod. Expert metal finishers know how to shape, file and weld metal so little lead or body filler is needed. The weld is laid a little at a time and the metal is tapped with a pick hammer and repeatedly filed to get a smooth shape. This process is time consuming, but isn't mandatory. Some body filler will not reduce the quality of the paint or bodywork.

Stripping the body

The first step in working with metal bodies is to strip them down to remove rust, paint and tar. The stripping technique varies depending on what type of metal you are working with. The vast majority of cars are made out of steel and can be stripped in a variety of ways. Abrasive methods are the most popular with media blasting being at the top of the list.

Sandblasting is just one of many types of media blasting. Walnut shells, soda powder, graphite, plastic and glass beads are just a few of the choices. Different media is used depending on the type of metal being stripped. Sand is the least expensive and is frequently used on steel. Most sandblasters cost around $400 and are ideal for stripping both old paint and rust. Sandblasting requires a lot of compressed air, so most of the small air compressors struggle to keep up. The job can be done with a small compressor, but you usually have to blast for a few minutes and stop as the pressure builds back up. Sandblasting creates enough heat to warp the outside panels and should not be used there, but it is perfect for firewalls, jams, trunks, floors or any other reinforced piece of steel.

A word of warning: Inhaling the dirty air and silica dust caused by sandblasting can lead to the breathing disorder known as silicosis. Always wear a helmet, gloves, suit and respirator while sandblasting.

Grinders and abrasive disks are also used to remove old paint and rust. A grinder with a 36-grit pad works well on outside panels and cuts paint quickly. There should not be a problem with the panels warping as long as you constantly move around the panel to distribute the heat. The grinder will take off good metal, too, so as soon as you see steel, stop and switch to a dual-action sander with an 80-grit pad. An assortment of wire wheels and abrasive disks are offered as drill or die grinder attachments for places the large grinders can't get to. A good grinder costs around $135 and can be used as a buffer, too.

Chemical stripping is another method at your disposal. "Chem dip" is the term used to describe the method of dipping the steel down into an acid bath to remove paint and rust. Some companies have chemical tanks so large that the entire body can be submerged. The process costs around $1,300 for a complete car body. The advantage with this method is that the rust-removing chemical gets into all the cracks and places you can't see. The problem with chemical dip is that you have to haul the car around and not all areas have a shop with this service. Also, the metal will begin to rust again fairly quickly, so you must be prepared to prime the entire body soon after it is removed from the acid.

Old-fashioned paint stripper is another chemical that is commonly used. Paint stripper will not remove rust, but is ideal for removing multiple coats of paint. The fumes are pretty noxious, so make sure you use a respirator and gloves to protect your skin. When working with aluminum, chemical strippers are a must. The metal is just too soft for abrasive means.

Which method is the best? The answer is all of the above, depending on the situation. If a car is extremely rusty, chemical dip may be your best solution. I don't use this method very often and hence recommend avoiding cars with that much damage in the first place. Sandblasting seems to work the best for the majority of situations, along with a grinder for the outside panels. If the paint buildup is excessive, time can be saved by loosening up the coats with traditional paint remover before the sandblasting takes place.

Minor rust can be repaired with a patch. First, the area is cut out. The inner portion of the body can then be cleaned out. The tool used here is a plasma cutter, but the job can be done just as well with an inexpensive cut-off wheel. Save the cut out metal as a pattern for the replacement part.

Tackling rust

Some degree of rust repair is usually unavoidable. The stripping process will remove surface oxidation and small pits. It will also help you assess the extent of the rust. Many of the areas you thought were pits actually turn to holes after they have been stripped. The smaller holes of ⅜ inch and less can be welded up. The excess weld can be ground smooth to complete the repair.

As the holes get larger, patch panels will need to be made and welded in place. The rusted area is first cut out and a new piece is made out of stock sheet metal. As with any welding on a car body, the piece is first tacked into place and welded slowly into place ¼ inch at a time. Between each small weld, stop and cool the area down with compressed air. This technique keeps the surface of the steel cool and reduces the risk of warping the panel. As the holes continue to get larger, the strategy for repair changes. For example, if the entire lower portion of a door is rusted through, it may be more economical to spend $300 and buy a new door.

It's common to find floor pans with holes 10 inches wide or more. This happens when cars aren't stored properly and water is allowed to collect inside. The most challenging aspect of floor pan replacement is removing the old pan without damaging the surrounding braces or floor supports. To master this type of repair, it helps to understand how cars are manufactured.

Steel bodies start out as flat sheet metal. These sheets are stamped into shapes and are spot welded together to form basic parts and these parts are in turn spot welded together to form the body. Looking at our floor example, inner and outer rocker panel sheets are spot welded together to form a boxed rocker panel. Individual sheets are stamped into the floor pans and laid on top of the rockers. Various braces and floor supports are stamped out and spot welded under the floor and so on. All of these individual components are spot welded together to create the floor. As the floor moves down the assembly line, other similarly created parts are welded on, like the firewall, fenders and roof. This process can be reversed, right down to hammering all the individual parts back to flat sheet metal.

If a floor pan is to be replaced, the spot welds holding the pan to the rockers and floor braces must be located and separated. Special drill bits can be purchased that drill out these small welds. Once all of the welds holding the panel in place have been removed, the panel will come right out. Replacement panels can be custom made or obtained from donor cars. Trim the replacement panel to fit and weld it in place using a spot welder, or weld up the drilled-out holes.

You may find yourself in a situation where you remove one rusted panel, only to find the adjacent panels and bracing to be rusted through as well. Professionals call this "Swiss cheese" because you remove one slice with holes in it, just to see the same thing on the next. You may end up drilling out 50 welds or more just for one floor pan, and it is tedious, time-consuming work. Add to this rocker panels, floor bracing and trunk flooring and you have a major commitment on your hands. If the holes are small, they can be welded up and ground smooth. However, if the next layer of steel has rusted to the point that it needs to be replaced, you may be fighting a loosing battle. It is very rare that one isolated

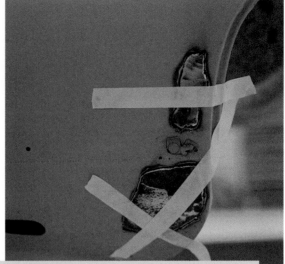

A replacement patch can be made with almost any scrap metal. Try to find scrap that is the same gauge as the original area. The patch can be held in place with a welder's magnet or "low-tech" masking tape.

brace or support has rusted through. Usually, if you find Swiss cheese in one place, it is all over the car, and the expense in repairing this is greater than the car is worth.

If you are committed to a body that is rusted to this degree, there is one fiberglass technique that may help you. Providing that the metal still has structural integrity, fiberglass can be set on the inside of a brace or rocker panel to give the metal strength and fill large rusted spots.

Let's use a rocker panel as an example. The rocker is the boxed piece of metal that runs down the length of the body just below the door. There is a rocker on either side of the car and it reinforces the body like the frame rails do. Some rocker panels have holes cut in them during the manufacturing process, and these holes allow water and salt to get up inside the body. In time, the rockers can deteriorate to the point where hundreds of little rust holes run down their entire length. To use fiberglass properly, access holes will need to be cut on the top side of the rocker. Both the inside and outside of the rocker need to be sandblasted and primed in epoxy primer. This will keep the metal from rusting again. Once it's dry, several layers of fiberglass resin and mat are laid on the inside of the rocker. Masking tape or wax paper can be used to keep the resin from dripping through the holes and onto the floor. Once dry, the excess resin can be ground flush on the outside of the rocker with a dual-action sander and primed again. This technique builds strength and fills the holes at the same time and is about four times faster than welding. The preferred solution would be to replace or weld up the metal, but fiberglass works well on a budget.

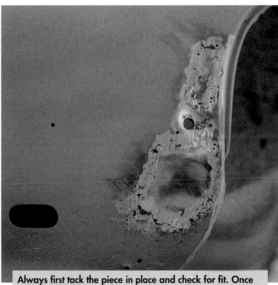

Always first tack the piece in place and check for fit. Once you're satisfied, finish the weld slowly and grind the welds flush for a finished repair. A droplight can be lowered behind the panel to see if any pinholes were missed. These can then be welded up fairly quickly.

Body modifications

The most common body modifications are chopping, channeling and frenching. Many of the modifications were first done to lower the car to the ground, reduce wind resistance and increase speed.

Chopping is a technique used to lower the roof of a car several inches and is one of the most popular modifications done today. Channeling removes the metal on the floor and firewall that is in contact with the frame. The entire body is lowered around the frame and welded in place. This modification lowers the body to the ground without modifying the chassis. Frenching is more of a decorative or

A hammer and dolly only work when you have access to both sides of the steel. Here, the body man is taking advantage of a removed quarter panel. He can now access both sides of the door jam and hammer out some accident damage. The dolly is placed behind the metal so the metal works flat as you tap instead of denting in.

An assortment of hammer shapes are needed in bodywork. This shape is perfect for getting behind a curved area.

styling. To create a custom look, taillight or turn signal housings can be removed, and the lenses grafted right into the body. This can be done with almost any exterior bezel or handle to clean up the body lines and get almost any custom design.

Another way rodders alter the appearance of a car is to build new panels from scratch. Famous examples of this would be some of the cars made for television, like the Batmobile. This car started with a stock body and then new panels were made for it to give it a truly unique look. Most street rods are not that radical, but custom-made hoods and hood panels are quite common.

When grinding down welds be sure to take a little metal off at a time and let the metal rest between grinding passes. This will help keep the heat down and keep the panel from warping.

Dan Kemppainen at Kemps Rod and Custom in Iron Mountain, Michigan, builds everything from show-quality street rods to their own limited production models, like the "Kempster." The techniques used to chop tops changes depending on the contour of the body. The next series of photographs show the chop process for three common body styles: '50 Mercury, '37 Chevy and '29 Model A.

Cutoff wheels are one of the more common bodywork tools. They cut straight lines with a minimum amount of heat. They are used to remove sheet metal and grind down welds.

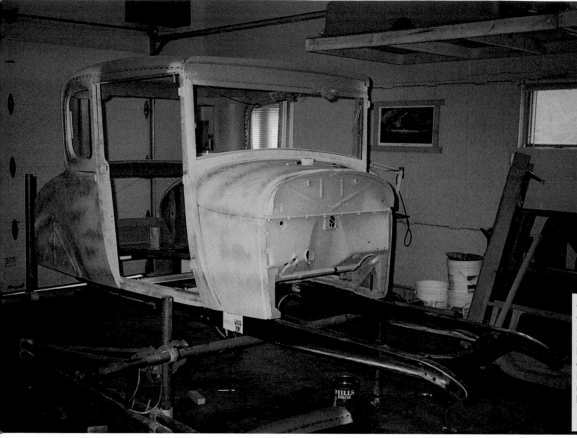

An early model T or A chop is one of the simplest chops to do. Since the window posts line straight up and down, less modification is needed to make the roof align once it is lowered. *(Kemps Rod and Restoration Inc.)*

For a 2-inch chop, measurements are made at the center of the window posts. The metal is then removed with a reciprocating saw. *(Kemps Rod and Restoration Inc.)*

The firewall has been replaced with flat sheet metal. It also has been modified to fit the distributor. This is just another reason to build a mock-up of the car before any serious bodywork begins. *(Kemps Rod and Restoration Inc.)*

As the welds come together, note that the window frames of the door have not been completed yet. They are done last.
(Kemps Rod and Restoration Inc.)

After the welds are ground down, normal body filler is used to smooth out the panel. Body filler can be put over bare metal, but it is better to prime the area first. Never put body filler over wash primer.
(Kemps Rod and Restoration Inc.)

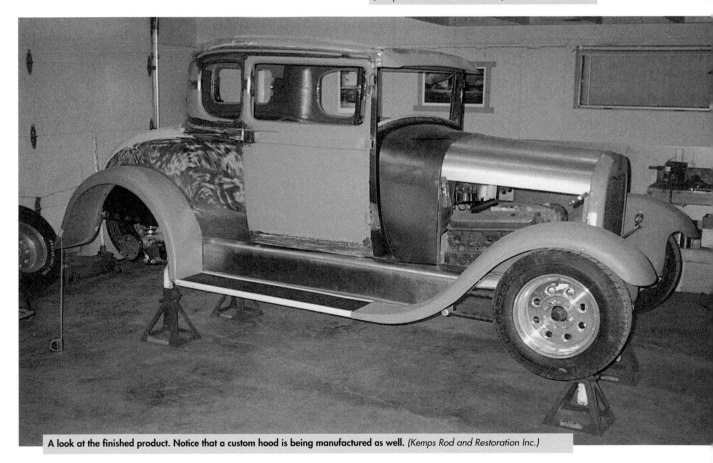

A look at the finished product. Notice that a custom hood is being manufactured as well. *(Kemps Rod and Restoration Inc.)*

The key to any successful modification is referencing. Whenever the dimensions of the body change, reference points are needed to make sure the body goes back together straight and level. In the case of chopping a top, the reference points are needed at the top and bottom of the window frames around the vehicle. The front window will get reference points at the top and bottom of either side of the window frame. A carpenter's square is first clamped perpendicular to the floor, and then the top and bottom reference lines are drawn on masking tape. It is important for the marks to be in line with each other. Take a top-to-bottom measurement between the lines. The distance between these two lines is exactly 15 1/2 inches. Logic follows that if we want a 3-inch chop, then the measurement should be 12 1/2 inches just before we weld the window post together. Reference points are placed and measurements taken on all of the windows and doors around the car. *(Kemps Rod and Restoration Inc.)*

The reference lines on the tape can clearly be seen. For added detail, the angle of the door window frames will be changed. Scribe lines on either side of this B pillar post mark the areas to be removed. A paper template is made so the lines can be duplicated on the driver's side. *(Kemps Rod and Restoration Inc.)*

Once 3 inches have been removed from the pillars, the entire roof will shift forward a couple of inches to mate back to the A pillar. To compensate for this forward shift, the rear window frame will be leaned down to make up the gap at the rear of the roof. *(Kemps Rod and Restoration Inc.)*

Cut lines are scribed so the rear window frame can be removed as one piece. *(Kemps Rod and Restoration Inc.)*

Before the roof pillars are cut, the door posts are removed. This will allow the roof to drop down. The driver's side reference lines can be seen on the front window frame. The roof provides substantial support and rigidity for the body—so much so that convertibles usually have a reinforced frame to compensate for the lost support. When the roof is cut loose, the body has a tendency to warp or change shape. It is important for the body to be bolted to the frame before any cutting begins. Notice the tube angled from the passenger door to the floor. This is an added brace that is tack welded to the floor and door jams to prevent the body from warping. *(Kemps Rod and Restoration Inc.)*

A typical roof weighs 200 lbs. or more, so a couple of adjustable roof supports are built out of scrap metal. This tool will support the roof while the posts are cut and hold it in place when it is time to weld. *(Kemps Rod and Restoration Inc.)*

As the roof drops down, the rear quarter glass will change shape. The window channels are cut away before the roof drops. *(Kemps Rod and Restoration Inc.)*

The roof is cut free at the "A" pillar posts and across the top of the rear window. A cutoff wheel and die grinder are used to make the cut. Weld gaps need to be kept to a minimum so a cutoff wheel thickness of 1/32 inch or less should be used. Once free, the roof is slid forward to mate with the "A" pillar. The reference lines are all checked to make sure the 3-inch chop is consistent all the way around. You can start to see how far the rear window will tilt down to mate with the roof. *(Kemps Rod and Restoration Inc.)*

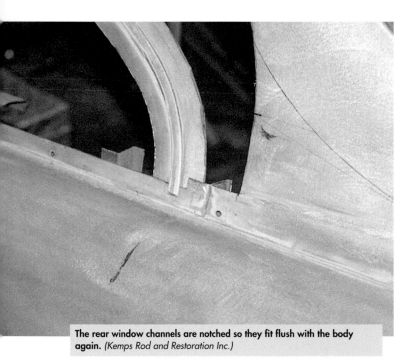

The rear window channels are notched so they fit flush with the body again. *(Kemps Rod and Restoration Inc.)*

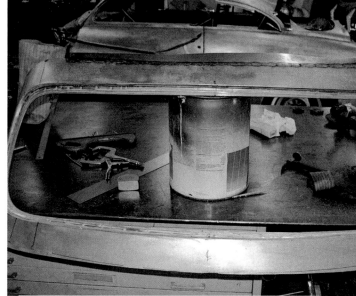

The entire rear window frame is cut loose. A test fitting of the frame at its new angle revealed that a 1/2- inch gap still exists between the roof and frame. A strip of metal is added to the top edge of the frame and will be trimmed to fill the gap. *(Kemps Rod and Restoration Inc.)*

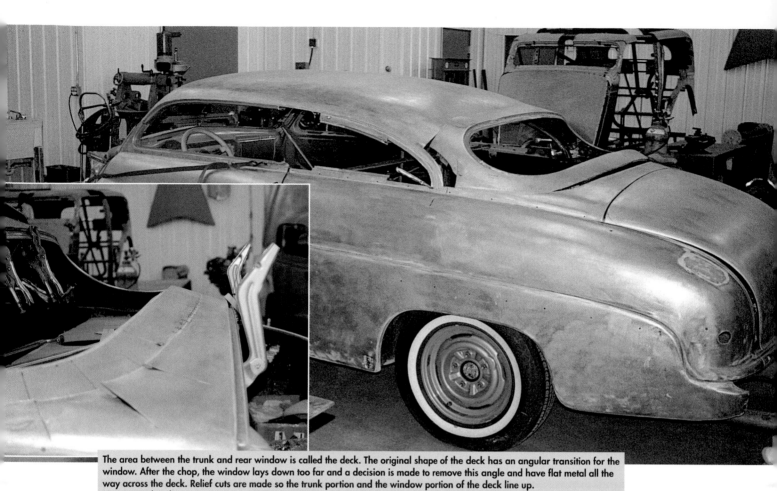

The area between the trunk and rear window is called the deck. The original shape of the deck has an angular transition for the window. After the chop, the window lays down too far and a decision is made to remove this angle and have flat metal all the way across the deck. Relief cuts are made so the trunk portion and the window portion of the deck line up.
(Kemps Rod and Restoration Inc.)

With the reference points checked, the rear window can be tacked in place. As the welds are filled, make sure the metal is not getting hot enough to warp the surrounding area. This is accomplished by welding small spots one at a time and cooling the metal with compressed air between each weld. *(Kemps Rod and Restoration Inc.)*

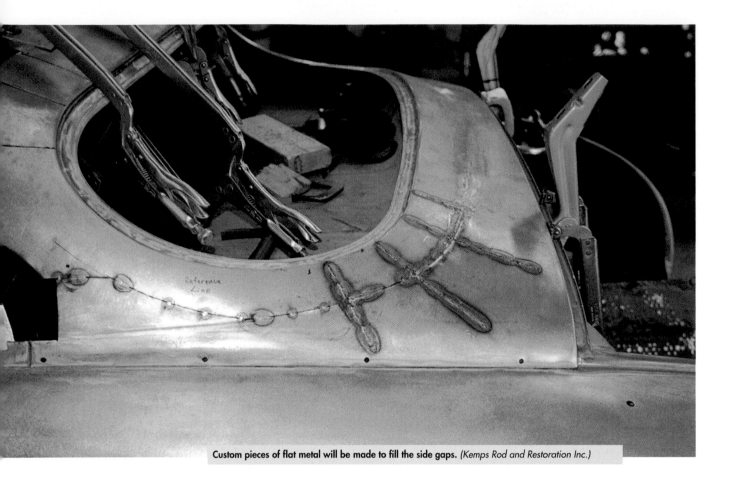

Custom pieces of flat metal will be made to fill the side gaps. *(Kemps Rod and Restoration Inc.)*

The transition between the roof and window frame is smoothed out the same way as the deck was done. Notice how the relief cuts are much longer. It is very easy to warp the roof with cuts of this length. Several reinforcements were welded from the door jams to the floor.
(Kemps Rod and Restoration Inc.)

Filler panels were manufactured out of stock metal and hammered to shape. There were so many relief cuts in the corners that it made more sense to graft in new metal than to weld up a dozen individual lines.
(Kemps Rod and Restoration Inc.)

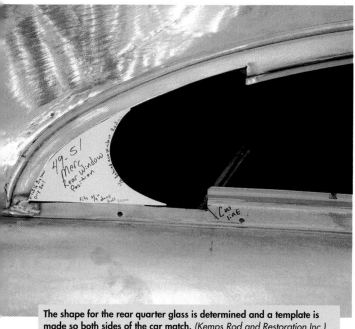

The shape for the rear quarter glass is determined and a template is made so both sides of the car match. *(Kemps Rod and Restoration Inc.)*

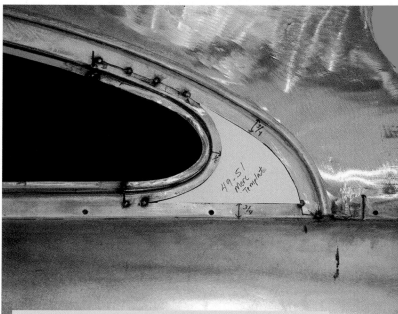

A piece of the original channel is trimmed and shaped using a stretching tool from Eastwood. It is tacked in place and checked. *(Kemps Rod and Restoration Inc.)*

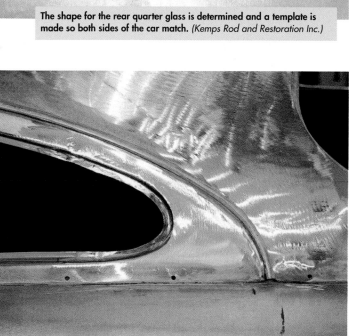

Once tacked, a small piece of flat metal is trimmed to fill in the gap behind the channel. Notice how the welds are almost impossible to detect after they have been ground flush. *(Kemps Rod and Restoration Inc.)*

The "B" pillar is angled forward to add detail to the body. The original posts were trimmed and stretched to fit the new angle. Once the posts have been welded in place, the body will be ready for bodywork. The greater the OEM angle of the front and rear windows, the more steps and work will be involved. This example represents one of the most elaborate and difficult chops you will encounter and costs around $15,000 if a professional does it for you. *(Kemps Rod and Restoration Inc.)*

Here is a '37 Chevy. The front and rear window frames on bodies of the late '30s have a moderate angle and are easier to work on.
(Kemps Rod and Restoration Inc.)

The chop begins with the same referencing as the Merc. Since this will be a 2-inch chop, masking tape is used to mark off the cut lines and reference points can be seen on both sides of the front window frame, as well as the rear quarter area.
(Kemps Rod and Restoration Inc.)

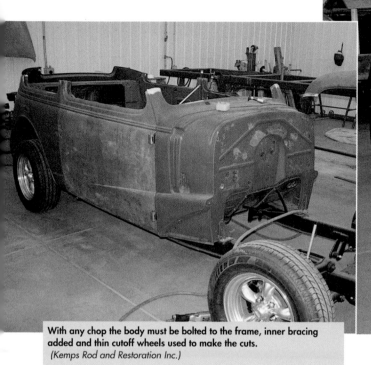

With any chop the body must be bolted to the frame, inner bracing added and thin cutoff wheels used to make the cuts. *(Kemps Rod and Restoration Inc.)*

The added brace from the door jams to the floor can be clearly seen. Since the rear window is almost perpendicular to the ground, the roof can be separated right through the center of the frame. A similar support should be made for the roof as it is lined up to the "A" pillar. *(Kemps Rod and Restoration Inc.)*

Once the roof has lined up, check the gap at the rear of the car before welding. *(Kemps Rod and Restoration Inc.)*

In this case, the roof is too far forward, although not as severe as the Merc. This should happen on any body where the front and rear window frames are at an angle. *(Kemps Rod and Restoration Inc.)*

Instead of leaning the rear of the car farther forward, a cut can be placed across the top of the roof. This allows the rear portion of the roof to slide back and mate up with the body. However, it leaves about a 1-inch gap across the roof. A narrow strip of steel is trimmed and TIG welded to fill the gap. Every effort should be made to weld slowly and keep the metal cool as you weld. Notice how a small strip of steel is welded along the door channel. This acts as a straight edge to keep the roof in line. (Kemps Rod and Restoration Inc.)

Even though the roof has been pulled back to mate with the body, the new roof contour is not smooth and the curve at the bottom of the quarter glass needs to be changed. Vertical relief cuts are made and the metal is slightly bent to get the correct contour. (Kemps Rod and Restoration Inc.)

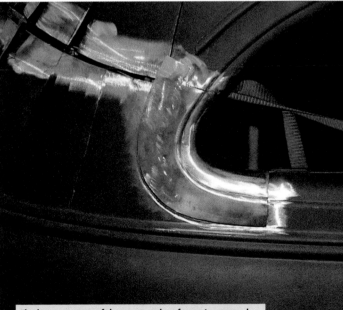

The bottom corner of the quarter glass frame is removed and reshaped to match the new contour.
(Kemps Rod and Restoration Inc.)

The overall welding process is similar to the Merc in the sense that the welds start at the "A" pillar and move to the rear. The center roof strip is welded next and the doors last. Your reference points should be checked repeatedly. *(Kemps Rod and Restoration Inc.)*

With the door frames welded in place, the overall chop is complete. This example has a moderate difficulty level and would cost around $8,000 in a shop. *(Kemps Rod and Restoration Inc.)*

Custom fabricated hoods and hood inserts are very popular and add detail to the overall design. This '35 Plymouth has an aluminum hood that opens as one piece to the passenger side. The hood inserts on either side are also fabricated out of aluminum with custom stainless stripes. *(Kemps Rod and Restoration Inc.)*

A project like this starts with aluminum sheet stock. The two hood inserts are clamped together and cut out at the same time. Since the hood will be shaped, the aluminum sheet is annealed first to reduce brittleness and ease construction. To anneal aluminum, take an acetylene torch and blacken the metal with the oxygen turned off. Continue to heat the metal until the black stains burn off. This is the exact temperature that aluminum anneals, and this process only has to be done once. Once cool, the metal will bend and shape easily without cracking. *(Kemps Rod and Restoration Inc.)*

The new hood is bent to the desired angle by hand. It has a trapezoidal shape from front to back. It takes experience to bend pieces like this, but cardboard templates can greatly simplify the process. The shape is fine tuned through good old trial and error. It takes patience and perseverence to get it right. *(Kemps Rod and Restoration Inc.)*

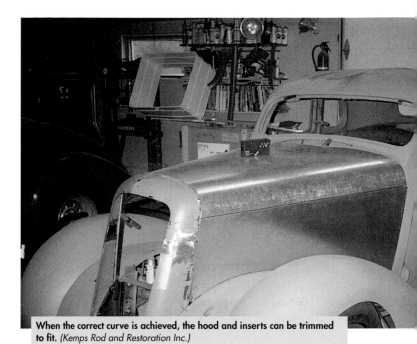

When the correct curve is achieved, the hood and inserts can be trimmed to fit. *(Kemps Rod and Restoration Inc.)*

In this case, the beautiful end result seems to have justified all the time and effort required to make the custom hood. *(Kemps Rod and Restoration Inc.)*

Chapter 9

Bodywork

A lot of steps go into making great bodywork. Complex areas often require creativity, imagination and patience.

MOST PEOPLE THINK THAT A GREAT PAINT JOB lies in either the quality of the painter, type of paint used, or number of paint coats. This is not the case. I can take an average painter with fair quality paint, combined with a top-notch body man, and get an outstanding paint job. However, you can take an ace painter, mix him with a second-rate body man, and the paint job will look terrible. High-quality bodywork is always the key to outstanding paint work.

Try to think of paint as nothing more than colored, shiny primer and you will have the right frame of mind. If dents are not repaired or the panels are wavy, the paint will only magnify the problem and make the mistakes easier to see. The primer on top of the body must be straight in order for the paint to look right. Notice that I did not say that the body has to be straight. No matter how good the metal or fiberglass work is, the body is never perfectly straight. Body men use lead or polyester fillers combined with primer to sculpt the body to perfection. The art form they use is called block sanding.

We can define block sanding as the process of repeatedly sanding a panel to remove defects in the body. Proper block sanding is the secret professionals

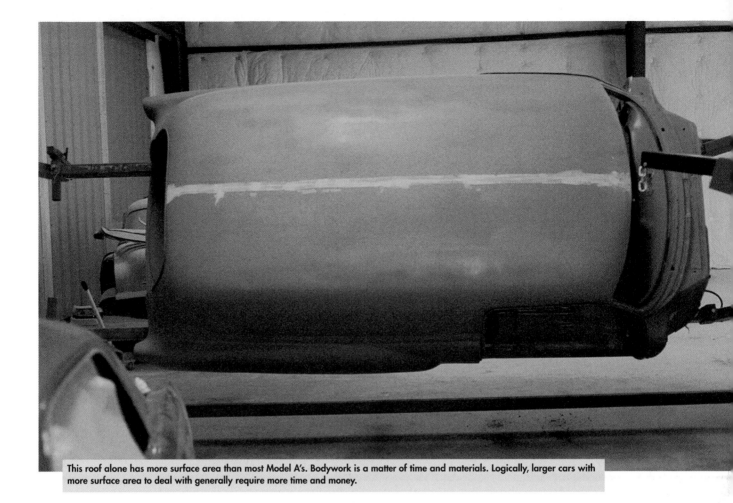

This roof alone has more surface area than most Model A's. Bodywork is a matter of time and materials. Logically, larger cars with more surface area to deal with generally require more time and money.

use to get incredible looking paint. The next time you stand at the front of a car, look down its side and move slightly from right to left. As you move, look at the objects being reflected in the paint. Do they flicker, flutter, or dance in the reflection? The surface should reflect a clear, steady image of the surrounding area. If the panels have not been blocked properly, the reflection will be wavy and distorted.

In this chapter, we'll examine the techniques used in block sanding. Top-notch paint and body men get paid well for a reason. Blocking takes time, patience, physical effort and skill. The first step is understanding how the different chemicals, materials and tools are used.

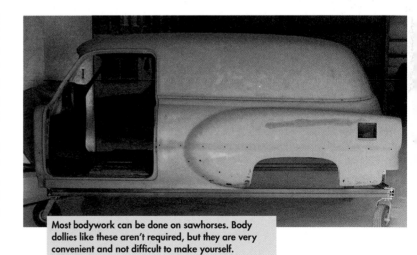

Most bodywork can be done on sawhorses. Body dollies like these aren't required, but they are very convenient and not difficult to make yourself.

Tools of the trade

Fortunately, the tools are not numerous or expensive. You will need an assortment of blocks, most of which you can make yourself. The sandpaper used in blocking is available through 3M and comes in a continuous roll. The paper is torn off to the length you need to match your block, but the width is always the same. The purpose of the block is to support the paper and keep it flat so you do not sand primer or body filler out of the low areas on the panel.

I frequently find myself making a new block every time I tackle a new project and over the years I have collected dozens of blocks. For example, a standard 12- or 18-inch flat block can be purchased from almost any automotive paint supplier. They

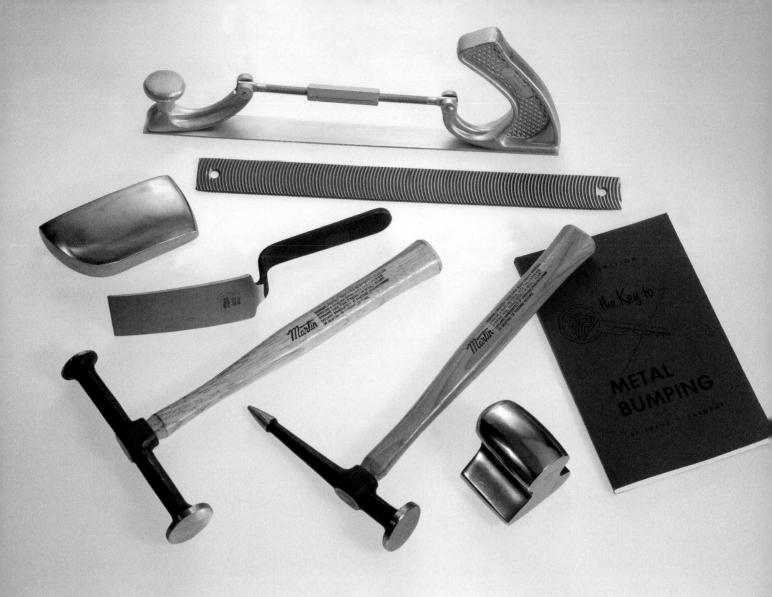

A wide array of body tools are used to straighten metal panels and fix dents. Special hammers, dollies, files and slapping spoons are sold separately or in sets. These tools are not cheap, but they are necessary for anyone planning to tackle their own bodywork. *(Eastwood Company)*

are usually made out of plastic and have convenient handles to hold on to. These are a good start and I recommend purchasing them.

You may find yourself with a narrow, concave shape that needs blocking. The top of the quarter panels of a late '60s Camaro have such an odd shape that a flat board-like shape will not fit down in such a curve. To solve the problem, I found myself making a block out of discarded rubber hose. Bingo, now you have another block in your collection.

In addition to blocks, you will need an air compressor and a primer gun. It is important to have filters on your air lines to remove condensation and oil from any air that will be used to spray paint or primer. It is during this phase that you first get exposed to the airborne chemicals and fumes that can cause health problems. It is important to isolate yourself from chemicals like primer and the best way to do this is to wear gloves, eye protection and a

government-approved air respirator.

I would recommend going even one step further if you intend to do your own bodywork and purchase a hooded suit and an outside air supply unit. The suit is not expensive, but the air unit costs around $1,000. This unit pumps fresh air into your suit and is the only way to fully isolate yourself from the harmful chemicals found in urethane primer.

Two tools that are not mandatory, but are great time savers, are a dual-action sander (DA) and an air file sander. Both of these tools use air to drive a high-speed sanding surface. The DA has a 6- or 8-inch circular pad and the file sander has a straight 16-inch pad. Both cost around $200. They save time on all of the initial body sanding, but get less useful as you begin to fine tune the panel.

Saw horses are useful when blocking, priming or painting removable panels like hoods, doors, fenders, etc. You can make them yourself out of wood

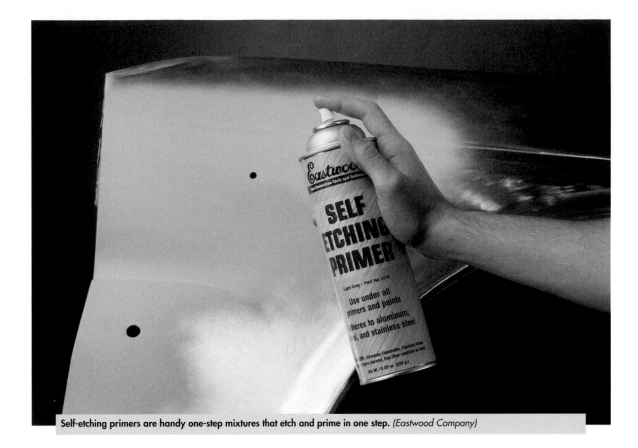

Self-etching primers are handy one-step mixtures that etch and prime in one step. *(Eastwood Company)*

with only a nominal investment. Some professionals use a more complicated saw horse called a body dolly or jig. These are made out of metal and vary in size from some small enough to hold a fender to others designed to hold and rotate an entire car. Even though they are useful, I would not encourage the investment unless you intend to paint many cars.

There are a few terms you need to know to make sense of the different materials and their labels. The first is substrate; defined in a dictionary as "the material or substance on which an enzyme acts" or "an underlying layer." When paint companies use this word, what they really mean is "the surface you are about to apply something to and what it is made of." If you are spraying primer on an engine block, then the substrate is cast iron. The substrate on a fiberglass car body is not fiberglass, it is gel coat. If you sand through the gel coat then the substrate is both gel coat and fiberglass. Also, if the surface has been primed, then the substrate is the primer, not the metal underneath.

Primers and surfacers

There are two liquid chemicals used in bodywork: primer and surfacer. Primers are chemicals that adhere to the initial substrates: steel, iron, gel coat, aluminum, fiberglass, etc. Only enough primer to cover the substrate one time is needed to do the job. I will refer to this as one coat. That does not mean that you will spray one pass over the surface to create one coat. Primers are very thin. You will need to spray them in light, see-through coats to prevent runs. You may need to make two or three thin passes over the substrate before one coat can be applied.

Surfacers are designed to be applied over primers. They are used to build material thickness for sanding and to provide a surface for paint to adhere to. Some paint companies offer products called primer/surfacers. These are surfacers that have bonding characteristics like primer. What can be confusing is the paint manufacturers use the proper terms, but the professionals often call everything "primer." If you hire someone to do your bodywork, the term "primer" is loosely used and if you do your own bodywork, you need to be specific in what you ask for at the paint store. If you just ask for primer, there's no telling what you'll get.

Different primers are used depending on the substrate and stage of bodywork you're in. Self-etching or wash primers have acids in them that chemically bond with various metals. There is no reason to use these primers on fiberglass. Different wash primers are used depending on the metal. Aluminum uses an etching primer called alodyne. It has a chromic acid base and is normailly wiped on. Most paint companies have a second wash primer that is used over the alodyne. Etching primers are mandatory

Primer needs around 24 hours to cure properly. Epoxy primers work well against most metals and fiberglass.

Early in the bodywork stage, bare metal is common. Wash, self etching and epoxy primers are all suited for bare metal applications.

When welding in panels, a hammer and dolly are frequently used to smooth out waves in the panel. The slower you weld, and the less heat you allow to build up, the less warping in the panel you will get.

When welding, frequently check the panel for heat. If it's warm to the touch, stop and wait for the panel to cool. Most welders weld a 1/4 inch at a time.

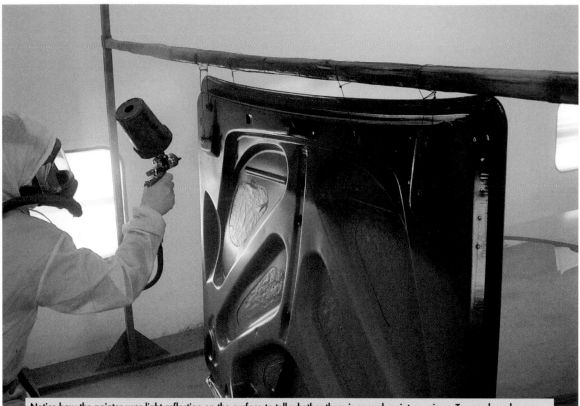

Notice how the painter uses light reflection on the surface to tell whether there is enough paint or primer. Too much and a run will develop. Likewise, if it is too dry, the surface will be rough and unattractive.

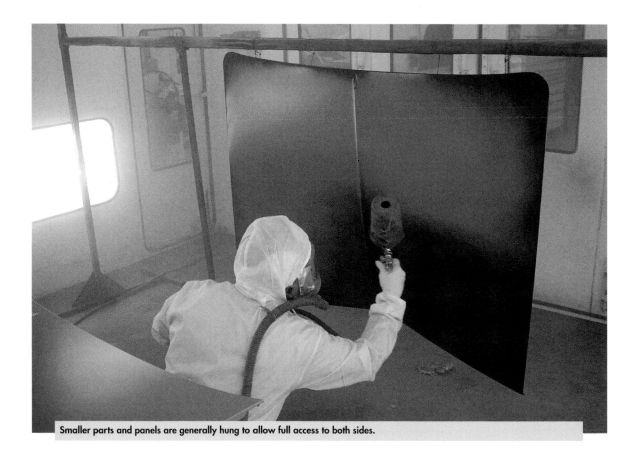

Smaller parts and panels are generally hung to allow full access to both sides.

Priming is a good way to practice spraying techniques. If you get runs, it's no big deal because you will be sanding the surface anyway. Always start in the hard-to-reach places like overhangs. Spray the panels last.

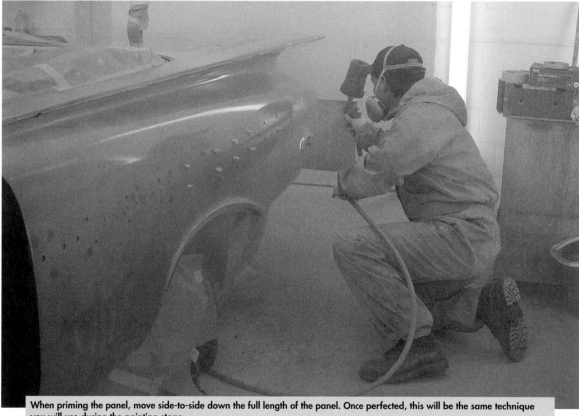

When priming the panel, move side-to-side down the full length of the panel. Once perfected, this will be the same technique you will use during the painting stage.

When applying primer, the car has to be masked off as if paint were being applied. This keeps primer out of unwanted areas like engine, interior, and trunk compartments.

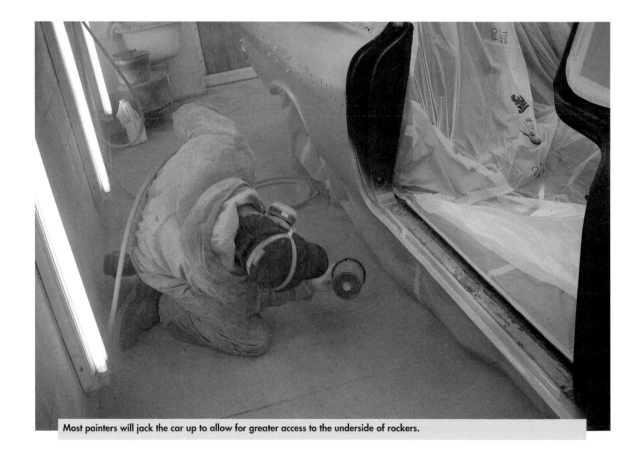

Most painters will jack the car up to allow for greater access to the underside of rockers.

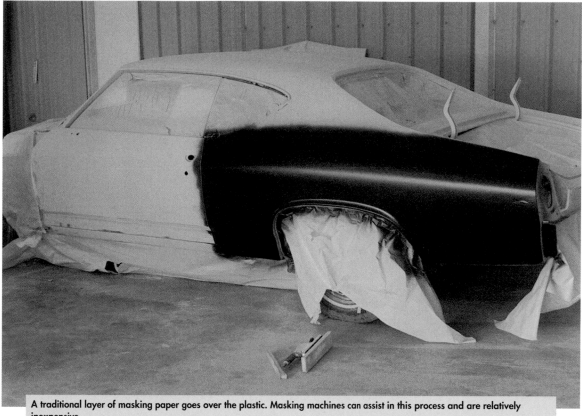

A traditional layer of masking paper goes over the plastic. Masking machines can assist in this process and are relatively inexpensive.

when working with aluminum.

Stainless steel requires a similar process, but skips the alodyne and starts off using zinc chromate primer. I've tried applying other primers straight to stainless, but it peels right off. Iron and steel work better with phosphoric acid. This acid has a unique quality that attacks rust very quickly, but is very mild on the rest of the metal. This is not to say that they should be applied over visible rust, just to point out that tiny rust particles will be destroyed by the acid. Steel-oriented wash primers generally use phosphoric acid as the reducer. This primer is not mandatory for steel or iron. It is typically used on metal that was not sandblasted or sanded with a dual-action sander. I recommend its use if the bare steel has been exposed to air longer than 24 hours after it has been stripped. This is a "just in case" measure to neutralize any oxidation that can't be seen with the naked eye. All etching primers are applied thinly and only require one coat. If applied properly, you should be able to see the metal through the primer.

None of these primers protect the surface from moisture for any length of time and they weaken or peel under heat. It is not recommended to use any kind of body filler over them as the heat produced during the curing process can damage the primer. If you choose to use wash primer, apply no more than what is needed for coverage and follow by applying

a coat of epoxy primer before moving on to other steps. You normally do not need to sand, prep or scuff the etching primer before epoxy. You just spray the epoxy right over the wash primer. This spray process is called "wet-on-wet."

Epoxy primers are useful because they do not react with acid-, lacquer- or enamel-based primers. They are chemically neutral, so they are used to seal old paint, primer, bodywork or fiberglass. Epoxy is both heat and chip resistant, so it is perfect for chassis components, radiators, engine blocks, inner fender wells or any other areas that may take a lot of abuse. Epoxy is water resistant, so it provides good protection for parts that may sit for a while before paint. It does not hold up to extended sunlight exposure, so you cannot store the parts outside, but it will protect metal from condensation and humidity.

High build primer/surfacers are used to cover bodywork and fill in low spots during the block sanding process. High build primers are designed to be thick, so they don't flow out of normal paint guns well. Most painters have at least three spray guns. Two of the guns use a 1.3mm tip. One gun is for sealers or single-stage paints, and the other gun is used for clear coats only. This helps keep the clear coat clean and free of colored contaminants. The third gun is used for primer and uses a larger diameter tip. I've seen tips ranging between 1.8 and 2.3mm depending

To prevent fisheyes, primed surfaces must first be cleaned with wax and grease remover. Then the surface is gently blown off with air and rubbed with a tack cloth. The tack cloth removes fine dust particles just before primer or paint is applied.

on the painter's personal preference. The larger the diameter, the more material will be applied with each pass.

Since all of the different primers touch each other, it is a good idea to use products from one paint line or manufacturer. Mixing different manufacturers, brands and lines is one of the most common reasons for paint failure amongst "do-it-yourself" paint and body men.

Body filler

Polyester body filler has gotten a bad rap over the years. There are multiple brands and they are all very similar. Bondo is a highly recognized name brand, and it seems that at every show I hear people talking down about the product. Bondo has the same quality as any other polyester filler, but since it is sold in almost every auto parts store, people who know nothing about paint and bodywork have access to it and use it incorrectly.

All polyester filler products are hygroscopic, meaning they absorb water. After these fillers are applied, they cannot be wet sanded or stored outside. The filler will absorb water and cause the steel underneath to rust. I have often stripped cars and found rust under body filler. This is why I recommend applying a coat of epoxy first to provide

a barrier between the metal and filler. Most labels will tell you it's OK to apply filler over steel, but why take a chance?

Body filler can be found in two forms: a spreadable paste, or a liquid that can be sprayed out of a primer gun. Both types have a hardener and it is important that the hardener get mixed into the filler thoroughly. If it is not mixed right, the filler can lift off of the surface later on. I can never say enough positive things about spray polyester. It is an incredible time saver. The blocking process is very repetitive because you continually apply primer over the panel and sand the material off. Spray polyester cuts multiple blocking cycles out of the project because its thickness fills in low spots better than ordinary primer.

Traditionally, body filler was rough sanded with 40-grit paper or a file and finished by hand. This technique can damage the surrounding area with deep scratches, so I recommend using this process only during the initial bodywork stages. As you fine tune, use a dual-action or power block sander with 80-grit paper to sand the filler close to flush. Finish sanding by hand in stages with 180- or 220-grit paper until the filler is smooth and the low spot can no longer be detected.

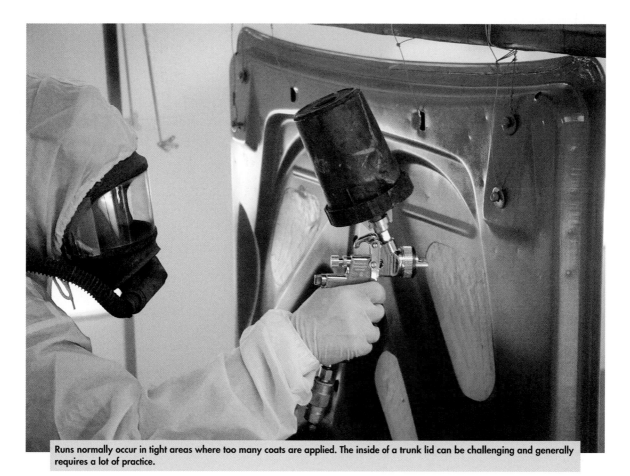

Runs normally occur in tight areas where too many coats are applied. The inside of a trunk lid can be challenging and generally requires a lot of practice.

Preparing for primer

Every painter is different, but I have a process I use that is the same for fiberglass and steel-bodied cars. Starting with the chassis, the components are sandblasted to remove rust, oil or paint. The surface is then blown off multiple times. Sandblasting cuts small pits into the steel that trap silica dust. One way to remove this dust is to wipe the entire surface with wax and grease remover and paper towels. However, wiping down an entire frame like this is time consuming. Scrubbing the metal with a Scotch Brite pad while blowing the surface with compressed air works just as well. One coat of wash primer and epoxy primer are applied and allowed to cure. Any pits or stamping marks are covered with polyester filler and sanded flush.

"Edge mapping" is a paint defect caused when the body filler absorbs chemicals out of the primer and swells. The risk of edge mapping can be reduced by sanding body filler with finer grits and coating them with epoxy before any further primer coats are applied. On chassis parts, two coats of epoxy primer can be applied over the bodywork and inspected to see if the repair is finished. You may need to repeat the process if the area still looks damaged, or a spot was missed. The epoxy can be wet sanded with 500-grit and prepped for paint.

If you are using a powder coat system instead of paint on your chassis, you should not fill or prime the steel. Powder coat is applied over bare steel only.

Outside panels

Bodywork on the outside panels of the car is more involved. After the steel has been stripped of paint and rust, the panels should be sanded with a dual-action sander using 80-grit paper. Take note of any dented areas that need repair. Dents that have easy access on both sides of the metal are tapped out using a variety of body hammers. The other side of the metal is backed by a dolly to prevent the metal from being tapped too far, thus creating a high spot. There are a wide variety of hammers available, but every body man seems to have a favorite. I find myself grabbing for a pick hammer without even thinking about it. Slapping spoons are usually used to work high spots. The metal is still backed by a dolly, but the spoon slaps the metal smooth so it is flush with the surrounding area. Body files are used to find subtle dents and remove slight high spots.

Dents that do not have full access will need to be pulled. The traditional technique involves drilling holes in the low spots of the dent. A slide hammer screwed into the hole and yanked the dent out. The problem with this technique is that it leaves multiple

This painter is fully protected from the spray environment. Gloves, paint suit, outside air supply and a full mask are needed to protect painters from the hazardous materials used in most automotive applications.

holes which need to be welded up. Spot-weld dent pullers were introduced to save time. With this technique small pins are welded to the low areas of the dents. The pins are placed every 3/4 of an inch or so. A special slide hammer is used to grab the pin and tap the dent out. When the dent is pulled, the pin is cut off and ground flush with the rest of the panel. Spot-weld dent pullers cost around $300 for a complete kit.

After the dents are pulled, the entire car panel should be rubbed with a Scotch Brite pad and blown with compressed air like the chassis was. Sandblasting leaves sand and dust in the cracks or joints of the body, so blow the car off repeatedly until no more sand is seen falling off the body. The outside panels should be wiped with wax and grease remover as an additional step. One coat of epoxy primer is applied to the entire body and allowed to cure. Polyester body filler is then applied over the dented areas and sanded flush with a block or dual action sander in stages with 80-, 120-, 220- and 320-grit paper.

You may want to explore the lost art of leading dents or low spots. Leading is fun, but isn't very practical. Extra care has to be given throughout the project to ensure that the panels are not exposed to heat. You take a big chance in warping the panels during the leading process. Molten lead is too hot to be applied over primer, so it cannot be used during the block stage.

You are probably familiar with the health risks associated with lead poisoning. I do not feel comfortable encouraging anybody to do something that leaves powdered lead in the environment. Polyester filler can do anything lead can do with less health risks and in a shorter amount of time. Polyester body filler, also called Bondo, is what most body men prefer. It is first mixed and then applied over cleaned areas. It bonds mechanically to the surface, so it is a good idea to rough up the surface with 80-grit sandpaper prior to application. I prefer to wipe the surface with wax and grease remover before every use.

The entire body should be blown off again and the sanded body filler cleaned with wax and grease remover. Epoxy is used to seal the sanded body filler and prevent edge mapping problems. Two to four coats of high build surfacer or spray polyester is applied over the epoxy with repeated coats applied to areas you intend to block sand, like the fenders, quarter panels, hood, etc.

How do you know when to use high build primers as opposed to spray polyesters? Spray polyesters build up thick and are great time savers during the blocking process. I usually use spray polyester on the exterior panels for two to three blocking cycles or until I see that the panels are getting straight. Once the panels no longer show any obvious high or low spots, I switch to urethane surfacer and start using a finer sanding grit like 180- or 240-grit paper. The purpose of shifting to finer grits as you fine tune the panels, is to reduce the chance of any sanding scratches showing themselves under the paint as the chemicals cure and slightly shrink over several weeks.

High build products usually go on heavy and some practice is needed to see how heavy the surfacer can be applied before it runs. One pass over the surface usually applies several coats at a time. Six to eight coats (not passes) are applied to the panels. Once cured, these panels are ready to be blocked.

It is important to note that the entire vehicle does not need high build primer/surfacer, only the areas that need to be blocked. Door jams, inside fire walls, door posts, and window sills rarely need to be blocked. Epoxy is usually suitable for these areas.

Blocking

The sides of your car are not smooth. They look more like the waves of an ocean with subtle high and low places. Blocking is the process of leveling these high and low spots so there is a uniform surface. Start by placing a thin guide coat over the surfacer to be blocked. While sanding, the guide coat will be used to measure where you are sanding surfacer off and where you are not. The places where the guide coat comes off quickly are the high spots, and the places where the guide coat is untouched are the low spots. A common guide coat technique is to mist spray paint over the surfacer. However, when sanded, the paint has a tendency to gum up on the sandpaper. 3M makes a dry-powdered guide coat that works better. The powder is smeared over the surface with a foam applicator. There is no wait time. The surface is ready to be block sanded as soon as the guide coat is applied.

If you were to take a piece of sandpaper in your hand and start sanding the guide coat, you effectively accomplish nothing. Your hand flexes with the contour of the low spots so you would sand surfacer out of the low spots as well as off the high ones. The panel would look the same. Block sanding uses file sandpaper backed by a "block," which is firm board. The block allows you to keep the paper flat over a longer distance. When sanding with a block, the surfacer is sanded off of the high area without touching the low spots. This is good, because you want the low areas to get filled in without excessive material buildup. A low spot might be a foot wide or more, so the length of the sanding board is important.

The board or block should be about half the length of the panel to be effective. If you are blocking a door that is 2 feet long, then the block should be about a foot long. Most hot rods have short panels as the cars of the '30s weren't very long, but as you move into the '50s and '60s, cars get upwards of 18 feet in length or more. Some quarter panels are at least 6 feet long, so an ideal block would be 3 feet long. File sandpaper is purchased in rolls so any length can be used.

After selecting a block, sand the surfacer with 120-grit paper at 45-degree angles from left to right several strokes and then switch and sand the other direction. Try not to press too hard against the panel as you do not want it to flex during the process. Constantly move around the panel so you are sanding around the panel equally. As you are sanding, watch the guide coat on the surface and take note of any places where metal shows up immediately. These areas are the high spots that will need to be lightly tapped with a pick hammer. Continue to block the panel until metal spots are showing in several places on the panel. The panel should be cleaned again in preparation for the next coats of surfacer.

Your next step is somewhat of a judgment call because there are different ways to handle low spots, depending on how deep they are. Place a straight edge over the low spot. If the area is more than $3/16$ inch deep, then the area should be treated as a dent. Panels that can be accessed from the back side can be tapped out or a dent puller used to work the dent out. For spots where the metal is close to $3/16$ inch deep, body filler can be used to fill in the low spots. Most of the areas will not be that deep, though. The more experience you get with this process, the earlier you detect the high and low defects. Ideally, you should be able to detect and address them before any surfacer is applied. That way you save material and money.

For the rest of the low spots, you can either apply more coats of high build surfacer or spray polyester filler. When you just spray material in localized areas it is called "spotting." Both of these chemicals can be spotted in the low spots. Block sand your body filler and spotted areas and clean the area again. The panels are sprayed again with six to eight coats of high build surfacer and the whole blocking process is repeated. There is no need to add more material to the structural areas like the jams or even the ends of the body—just the wavy portions of the exterior panels. If your blocking was done correctly, the high spots should take longer to show up and the low spots should all be filled or smaller. High build primer can be spotted in the low spots and the entire process is repeated as needed.

As you work through the blocking steps, the low areas should get smaller and smaller. You can test to

Initial block sanding quickly reveals high and low spots on body panels.

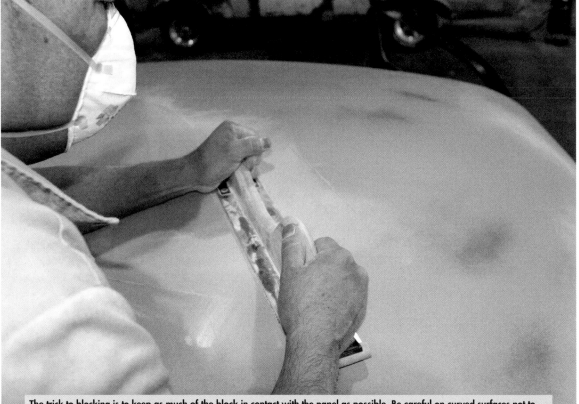

The trick to blocking is to keep as much of the block in contact with the panel as possible. Be careful on curved surfaces not to allow the block to gouge lines in the primer. *(Eddie Paul)*

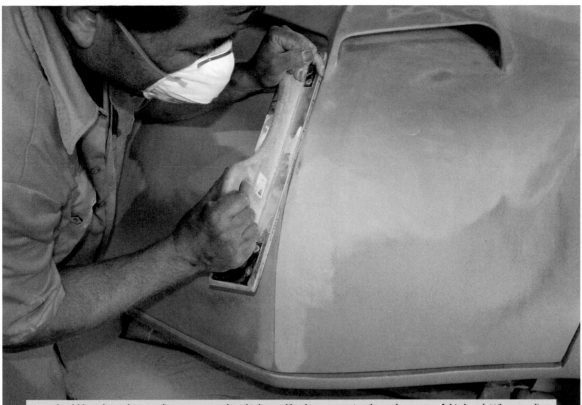

Care should be taken when sanding up to a peak or high spot like the one running down the center of this hood. When sanding the hood, do not stop at the base of the moulded peak; instead, your sanding stroke should continue up to the top of the peak. Otherwise, you will cut a line right at its base leaving an odd-looking edge. *(Eddie Paul)*

When applying filler to difficult-to-sand areas like this trunk lip, use a minimum amount. This will help reduce sanding labor afterwards. *(Eddie Paul)*

Sandpaper is available in both dry and wet styles. Wet sanding paper is generally used with the finer grits, like 400 grit and finer. *(Eddie Paul)*

During wet sanding, a constant flow of water is needed to move the sanded material away from the paper. This body man is using a water bottle. *(Eddie Paul)*

High-quality bodywork should be straight and dent free. To get a close look at bodywork, look down the length of the car and observe the reflection in the paint. The reflection should be free of distortion and waves.

see if a panel is finished by wiping the panel with wax and grease remover and looking at an image in the reflection. As you move your head from side to side, the image should stay steady and look smooth. If it is distorted or flutters, then the panel needs further blocking.

There will be several places where a traditional block cannot be used. You may need to fabricate custom blocks out of balsa wood or foam to address narrow areas or curved places around the edges of the body. A wide assortment of lengths and shapes will be used throughout the blocking phase. When it appears that the panel is close to being finished, switch to a less aggressive grit such as 220. Finish blocking the panels using 320-grit paper and double check the panel for straightness using wax and grease remover. You may find yourself going through four blocking sessions or more depending on the length of the vehicle.

When your bodywork is finished, lightly sand any overspray off the entire vehicle with 320-grit and wet sand the entire body with both 400- and 600-grit wet sanding paper. No bare metal spots should be showing. If you sand through the surfacer, spot in more surfacer or epoxy primer and wet sand your spotted areas again. The entire vehicle should be cleaned at least two times before moving on to paint.

Quality control is the customer's job

Bodywork is the most important step to a high-quality paint job. Not all professionals know how to do it right, either. All the word "professional" means is that a person does the work as their primary means of support. It doesn't mean that the individual has the necessary skill. To give you an example of how bad professional body work can get, I'll share a story about a '58 Chevy I worked on a few years back.

This particular car was brought to our shop because the previous shop and the owner had a falling out. This is not uncommon in the industry, so I wasn't suspicious of a problem right off the bat. The car body was painted, buffed and sitting on the chassis. All we needed to do was the final assembly work, and the customer agreed to our standard hourly rate. He had already spent $25,000 for rust repair, bodywork and paint, and I guessed we would need another $10,000 plus parts to finish the job. At first glance, the paint looked OK to me. It was buffed out nicely and the bodywork was close to straight so the job didn't seem like it would be that big of a deal. I honestly didn't sit down and pick over the car or check the panels with a magnet.

When it comes time to line up and install the stainless trim, I like to see how well the pieces fit to

Much of bodywork is fitting parts properly and blocking them to match. A beautiful paint job only reflects what is underneath. Notice how the reflection of the pavement line is wavy. This is because the panels were not blocked properly. Also, note how the exhaust isn't centered in the hole, and the bottom of the door sticks out slightly.

the car and line up. This is where the first problem popped up. None of the quarter panel trim would fit the car. Naturally, I assumed there was a problem with the trim, but these parts were in excellent shape. It was like they were for a different car because the curvature between the panels and the trim was completely wrong.

I stopped and studied the body of the car for a second and something else looked strange. A '58 Chevy Impala has little racing scoops stamped into the sheet metal just behind the door and this car didn't have those on either side. Up until this point, I had never seen really bad bodywork before, so my first thought was that we had some factory mistake and that we may have a very rare car on our hands. I briefly got excited!

So I looked inside the car through the hole that would contain the rear quarter glass and the stamping was visible on the inside of the panel. "What the … ? How is this possible?" Then I noticed

something else. In this same area, there is supposed to be a triangular brace that holds the convertible top piston to the floor. I could see where the brace had been, but it had been cut away from the floor. This also baffled me, because why would anybody of sound mind destroy or remove anything that has to do with the top mechanism? I decided to just stop and examine the car from head to toe.

After extensive study of the car, both inside and out, the mystery unraveled. This car had had extensive rust problems. Most of the floor was rusted away like Swiss cheese and covered with filler, the body mounts were gone and covered over, and the perimeter of the body had plates brazed over rust and covered over with slabs of body filler. There was no real metal supporting the portion of the floor that held the front seat. The customer could have gotten out on the highway and become intimate with the road, if you know what I mean. This car was a complete disaster! There were places where the body filler was over an inch thick. As the foreman, I had the unpleasant task of educating the customer that all of his $25,000 was wasted.

He then had to pay us to strip the car down to bare metal and start over again. At each step we would find some new disaster or challenge to overcome. I have never seen work this bad in my entire career. The customer stayed with us through the rust repair phase and through the point where the rear portion of the body got painted. However, by this time he had more than $50,000 spent and very little to show for it. He eventually ran out of money and had to sell the car at a huge loss.

I never had the heart to ask him what he got for the car, but I would guess he got less than $20,000 for it. I lost track of him over the years, but I heard the project damaged his marriage.

It's a sad story, but two very important lessons can be learned from this. First, it is your responsibility to verify the level of competency of the people you hire to work on your car. You are essentially a project manager and are no different from a foreman supervising the building of a bridge. If the bridge falls, management gets blamed and the individual workers disappear. What control will you have over the process? You need to make monthly visits and inspect all of the work as it is being done. Insist on daily or weekly photo documentation.

Second, you should see finished products or examples of the shop's work and talk to former customers before making any decisions. Incompetent people burn lots of bridges. Lastly, avoid and be suspicious of any requests for large deposits. Struggling shops will take in more work than they can handle to get the deposits to pay bills. Sooner or later the house of cards caves in.

Chapter 10

Paint

A great paint job can be subtle or stunning, complex or simple. Experience and attention to detail are crucial to achieving great results.

THE FIELD OF AUTOMOTIVE PAINT is surrounded in myth, mystery and misinformation. Car shows and swap meets are full of people giving advice who have never sprayed a drop of paint in their lives. Paint is the one area where advice should be taken from professionals only. A lot of people encourage hobbyists not to do their own paint work.

Obviously, painting takes skill. Professional painters at high-volume collision centers are well paid and for good reason. The skills they possess take time to learn and their jobs are difficult. Most of these skills are learned the old-fashioned way—through trial and error. We learn by making mistakes, but

painting mistakes are time consuming and expensive to fix. If a mistake requires repainting, a day is needed for the paint to dry, and then time is needed to sand the area smooth again. Professionals count all of the time needed to do this and many shops do not pay their employees for redo work. The material expense is also measured. A gallon of paint, with hardeners and reducers, can run upwards of $500, so numerous mistakes can rapidly eat any savings you may have had by doing the work yourself.

To limit rework expenses, I like to start new painters out on small parts like chassis or engine compartment components. The smaller parts use less

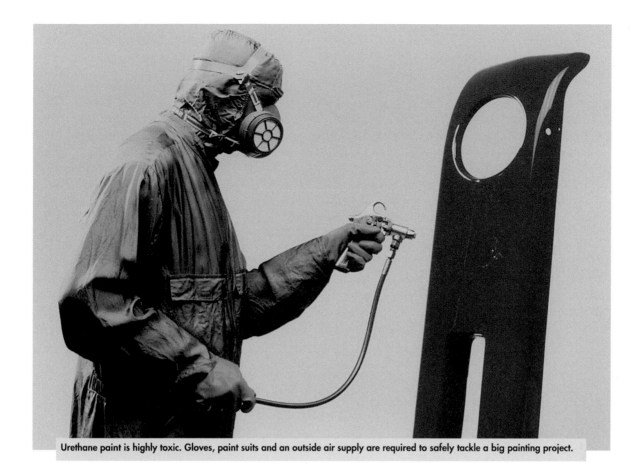

Urethane paint is highly toxic. Gloves, paint suits and an outside air supply are required to safely tackle a big painting project.

material and take less time to repair should a mistake be made. As your skills improve, you can move on to panels, like a door or fender. It may take several years to acquire enough skill to tackle a complete body, so patience is critical.

Modern paints are toxic and can pose a serious health risk if handled improperly—another reason why knowledge and experience are important. The paint needs to be sprayed in a clean, well-ventilated area. These concepts don't mix well because the faster you move the air in your painting environment, the more dust or contaminant gets stirred up and settles in your paint. In addition to air flow, safety equipment is needed to isolate you from the chemicals and this equipment can get pricey. New safety equipment can cost more than the initial paint job. The purchase is really only justified if you intend to paint several cars as an ongoing hobby.

High-quality paint work is expensive. If you opt to have a professional do both your paint and bodywork, you should expect bids between $6,000 and $20,000 to paint a car, depending on the quality of the finish and the size of the vehicle. If you do the bodywork yourself, you can cut these figures in half. Expensive? After you become familiar with the process and see what's involved, you may not think so.

Paint history

Lacquer paint has been in use for more than 600 years. It was used to finish furniture and temples as far back as 1397 in Asia. However, it wasn't until the turn of the 20th century that it became practical in industrial applications. Ford is mostly to thank for its refinement.

Lacquer dries very quickly and refinishers love it because it is easy to use and doesn't require expensive equipment to apply. When lacquer is sprayed, it lays down smooth, but doesn't dry glossy. Both manufacturers and refinishers have had to polish the paint to get it to shine. This process is slow and expensive, especially in an assembly line atmosphere.

Manufacturers sought ways to eliminate the polishing step and eventually introduced enamel paints that dry glossy, thus eliminating the manual polishing step. Refinishers and hot rodders resisted this paint through the '70s because enamels dry slowly and with a bumpy texture called "orange peel." Put a polished lacquer finish next to an unpolished enamel one and the lacquer would win the show every time. Enamels could compete only if you sanded the orange peel off and polished the surface like you do with lacquer. Since lacquer dries almost orange peel free, the entire enamel process takes longer, so why bother? Both paints deteriorate about the same when exposed to the sun.

In the late '70s, urethane enamel became popular because it dries almost as quickly as lacquer, is more durable, and has more depth to its shine. The drawback is that the catalyst in urethane paint is derived from cyanide and is highly toxic. Not knowing about the dangers, over the years many of the "old timers" continued to spray the paint using the same dust masks they used with lacquer. This proved to be dangerous and accelerated retirement for many of them.

Urethane eventually became the new standard, but not for application reasons. It has a low VOC (volatile organic compound) content. VOCs have been linked to air pollution and are closely monitored by the government. Lacquer has a high VOC content. Even if you wanted to use lacquer, chances are you wouldn't be able to find it because it is restricted and regulated in most states.

Urethane is the most common paint used in collision repair shops around the United States.

Paint basics

Paint is composed of four parts: pigment, hardener, binder and reducer. The pigment is the color that you actually see. Pigment is mixed into a clear binder, which is the liquid that makes up the majority of the paint. A hardener is added to the binder to create a reaction that cures the paint, and reducers are used to get the right viscosity so the paint sprays well.

The reducers are the main source of VOCs, so paint companies have been trying to reduce or eliminate their use. The most common way this is done is to use paints with a high solid content and special guns that can lay the thicker paint down with minimal reducer content. These guns are called HVLP (high volume/low pressure) and can be purchased for around $400. They shoot high solid paint well by breaking the paint spray into a finer mist than traditional guns and are designed to spray at 25 to 35 lbs. of air pressure compared to the 45 to 55 lbs. normally used. The lower air pressure reduces overspray and waste. Most auto refinishers are using high solid paint with HVLP guns.

Another way to reduce VOCs is to use waterborne paint. Waterborne paints use distilled water as a reducer and special hardeners to chemically bond the paint in a way that is similar to normal urethanes. VOC content is greatly reduced, but this type of paint is difficult to use and requires special equipment to spray. If you live in a state that requires its use, and everything else is outlawed, it's best to take your car to a professional (or another state). It just won't be

practical to paint the car yourself.

As a rule, I avoid waterborne paints. Ten years ago, it looked as if the whole industry was moving in that direction. They were all the rage, but as the years went by, I've seen them less and less. That usually means they weren't well received. I have had painters complain to me that they noticed a higher rate of failure with waterborne products as well. High solid/low VOC paint technology has taken over most product lines, and I have had better success with this style of paint.

Paint stages and what they mean to you

Automotive paint technology can be divided into three more subgroups or styles: single stage, base coat/clear coat and pearl coat. The style is mostly determined by the color you choose and it is important to understand these terms (styles) so you can order paint properly. Each of these requires slightly different application techniques.

Solid colors—ones without metallic flake—are usually applied as a single-stage paint, which means that the pigment, binder, hardener and reducer are poured into one can, mixed and sprayed in one step. Red, yellow, white and black are all common single stage colors. The advantage to single stage paints is that they are applied as one spraying step, which reduces the amount of time for airborne contaminants to settle down in the paint. If you intend to paint the car yourself and do not have a paint booth, you may want to pick a solid color to reduce contaminants in your paint (there's that planning thing again.) Solid colors are also easier to repair if you get a chip or deep scratch.

Two-stage or base coat/clear coat paint is applied in two spraying steps. The color is applied first in thin coats (called the base coat) and then followed with clear coats. The base coat dries quickly and is designed to allow the metal flake to lay flat against the car. The clear coats have the hardener and provide all the protective and durable qualities. A cleaner painting environment is needed because the application process takes longer with base coat/clear coat colors. Silver and gold are good examples of metallic paints that require paint to be sprayed in two steps.

Have you ever looked at a car and noticed that it changes colors depending on the angle you view it? This is called a pearl coat and it is applied in three steps. If you wanted a green car to shift to blue in the sun, then you would first apply a green ground coat. Then a special see-through pearl blue coat is applied, followed by traditional clear. Pearl colors are difficult to spray.

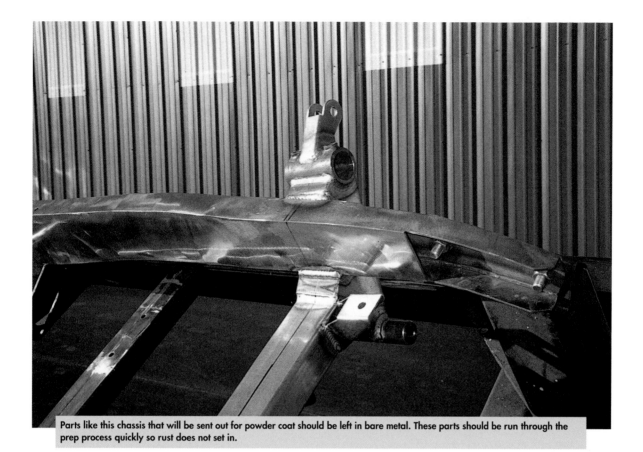

Parts like this chassis that will be sent out for powder coat should be left in bare metal. These parts should be run through the prep process quickly so rust does not set in.

Auto paint stores and most paint shops have volumes of paint chip books for you to thumb through to assist in color selection. It is expensive to change the color later on so take some time and make sure you have a color you like.

Powder coating

After the bodywork is finished, the body and frame can be separated. The painting process usually starts with the chassis, but the builder must decide if normal paint or powder coat will be used.

Powder coating is essentially a dry paint process. The pieces are electrically charged and a powdered paint is fogged over the steel. The excess powder falls to the floor and is reused. After the parts are coated they are baked in an oven at 400 degrees F. to cure the paint. Powder coating dries glossy, gives off low emissions because there are no liquid solvents, is chip resistant and does not peel when exposed to brake fluid.

You can get just about any powder coat color you want and you can buy do-it-yourself kits for less than $300. The kit comes with everything needed to coat parts small enough to fit in your oven. There is really no practical way to apply powder coat to the body of the car, but many rodders prefer it on chassis components because it is so durable. You could mix the application, too. For example, you could paint the frame and powder coat the smaller parts. Some people like to take the large parts to a professional and purchase some of their powder to use at home for everything else.

Powder coating has many advantages, but it cannot be used on rubber or plastic. Some control arms or leaf springs have rubber bushings and they will not hold up to 400-degree temperatures. This heat issue could affect your entire plan. For example, the chassis must be fully assembled to do your bodywork and some parts require bushings. Bushings are not fun to install and they are even more difficult to remove, so you may need to powder coat some of your parts before you assemble the chassis. These parts will need special attention throughout the project to avoid overspray and damage.

Also, you cannot use any type of body filler with powder-coated paint. Let's say your frame has all kinds of pits and hammer marks in the steel. If you use traditional paint, you can prime the frame and use body filler to smooth out the rough spots. With a couple more coats of primer, the steel will look new again. There is no practical work-around for this process in powder coating yet. Conventional paint has fewer planning issues to consider and may be the best choice for first-time builders.

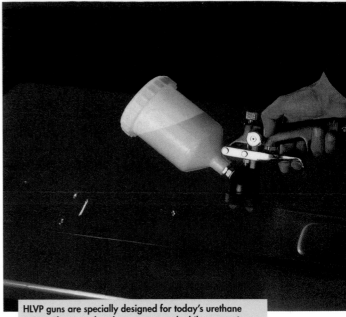

HLVP guns are specially designed for today's urethane paints. These produce less orange peel while conserving paint at the same time. *(Eastwood Company)*

A washable painting suit is a relative bargain at about $25. An air supply and gloves are also needed when working with toxic urethane paint. *(Eastwood Company)*

Safety

Urethane paint is not as easy to use as lacquer, but it can be applied by hobbyists. For health reasons, it requires the purchase of extra equipment to protect you from the chemicals. Gloves, goggles, paint suit and an outside air supply mask or respirator are required to isolate the painter from the toxins in the paint. This equipment costs between $1,000 and $2,000.

I've seen many outstanding paint jobs that were sprayed in garages. Keep in mind that sufficient airflow is needed to pull the overspray and fumes out and away from both you and the car. Most hobbyists will line their garages with clear plastic, wet the floor and use a box fan to pull the fumes out. The toxins are not the only hazard, however. All paints form a flammable mist when sprayed, so the fan absolutely must be an explosion-proof fan. These types of fans are sealed so the fumes do not come in contact with the motor.

Lastly, I think it is important not to paint alone. I know of a guy who was not using a proper respirator and passed out in the booth. Since the booth had no windows, he was on the floor quite a while before anybody found him.

Painting prep

Preparation is the key to good paint work. Before you begin, be sure to check the paint company's recommended preparation process. There are primers, surfacers and sealers. Some chemicals act as both. Technically, you can apply paint to any surfacer, but some brands insist on a sealer coat between the paint and the surfacer. This always makes me a little nervous because what they are indirectly telling you is that their paint line has inconsistencies so they need a barrier between their own chemicals. I avoid using brands like this.

Sealers have their place, however. During the sanding process, if you sanded through the surfacer

Mixing paint lines usually leads to trouble. Chemicals are designed to work together and can sometimes clash between brands. Whatever paint line you select, be sure to use that same company's primers. *(Spies Hecker)*

Do not store or mix paint inside your painting environment. This leads to an increased chance of fire and clutters your work environment.

A rotisserie can really ease the process from bodywork to paint. Without this tool, you can use saw horses to accomplish the task. I have seen some shops even fabricate an inexpensive rotisserie out of two engine hoists. (Street Rods by Michael)

What the rotisserie really assists in is the roof. It can be difficult to reach and spray this area without damaging or touching the wet sides of the car. (Street Rods by Michael)

and into old paint or primer, or if you are not using a primer that specifically says it is also a surfacer, then sealer is a good idea. If you sanded into some bodywork, then paint will usually show rings on the feathered edges of primer or body filler. This is called "bulls eyeing." Sealers are used to prevent this as well. A normal paint color will completely cover in three coats, but if you find you need more, then apply a coat of tintable sealer between the surfacer and base coat. Tintable sealers allow you to mix in some base coat with the sealer to die it close to the final color, and this saves time and material.

When you feel your bodywork is finished and the surface is ready for paint, it is important that the surface is free of any heavy-grit sanding scratches. To remove these, first clean the surface with wax and grease remover the same way you cleaned during the bodywork phase. Apply a light guide coat and block the surface with 240-grit dry sanding paper. If you break through the surfacer in several places, you will need to reapply surfacer and block with 240 again. When the panel is truly straight, you should be able to block with 240 without numerous or large break-through spots. Clean and lightly guide coat the surface again.

Every paint company is different, but usually the surface needs to be sanded with 400- to 600-grit wet sandpaper or 600- to 800-grit dry sanding paper. I prefer to wet sand with 500-grit paper. This process eliminates dirt nubs or orange peel in the surfacer as well as the previous 240-grit scratches. Wet sand the area until all of the guide coat is gone. Both hard and soft wet-sanding blocks can be used, depending on the contour of the panel. The surface should then be wiped down with wax and grease remover until your paper towel looks clean. This usually takes two times. Blow off the surface with compressed air and lightly wipe with a tack cloth at least two times. It is important to spend extra time blowing in any area

Scallops were some of the first designs found on hot rods. These shapes morphed into flames throughout the 1950s.

that might still have water left over from sanding. If your environment is clean and well ventilated, you are ready for the next step.

You may have some items you would like to mask off. Be sure to use both paper and tape that are designed for automotive refinishing. Some tapes have a resin that reacts with paint. Masking off a design like flames, stripes or scallops comes later. Mask off anything you do not want paint on at this time. If you touched the surface, then you will need to clean the surface again to remove any oils that may have come from your skin.

Normally, a coat of sealer is needed, so when the surface is clean, I like to blow the area off again and apply one coat of sealer. Sealers are designed to have paint sprayed right over the top of them without being sanded. This is called "wet on wet" or "non-sandable" sealer. You have a time window in which the paint must be applied and that is usually no longer than eight hours. Any longer and you will have to sand the sealer and apply a new coat.

Sealers are usually much thinner than the primers you used during bodywork, so spray them in light coats. I often refer to a light coat as a half coat. One coat should just be enough to completely cover the surface, so a half coat should be see-through. Only one complete coat of sealer is needed to do the job, but you will reduce or eliminate runs if this coat

is applied in half or even third coats, depending on how thin it is. Also, if you apply sealer in thin coats you will reduce orange peel that will be visible on the surface.

Paint application

As soon as the sealer has had enough time to flash off, the paint can be sprayed. Be sure to check the manufacturer labels for specific product information, because flash times differ between companies. Single-stage and two-stage paints are applied differently. The base coats are applied in thin half coats much like sealer until all of the sealer has been covered. Then apply two more half coats just to be safe, because it is easy to miss spots when wearing a full paint suit and helmet. This should ensure proper coverage. You may see some trash or dust in the paint. These particles will sand out of the top coats, but if the trash looks large, allow the base coat to dry (about 20 to 30 minutes) and lightly sand the contaminant and reapply base coat in that area. This is necessary because if the contaminant is too large, you will sand through the clear coat during the color sanding phase. To avoid this, lightly sand the particles with 1,000-grit paper, then clean and spray with base coat in those areas again. The base coat has a similar time window to the sealer (usually 8

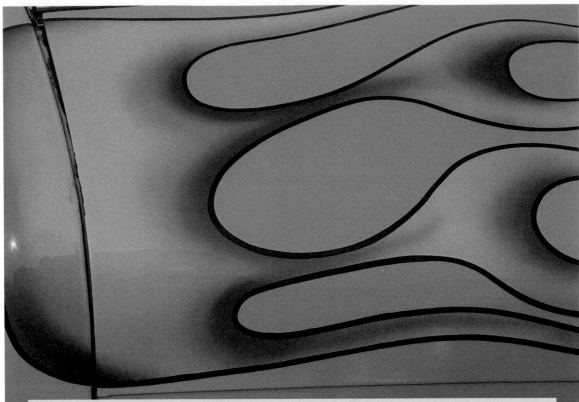

Multicolored flames require some thought and planning. Although a "patriotic" look can work, it may not be the best color choice for a yellow car. Also, the colors have to be sprayed with more reducer than normal in order for the colors to fade better.

Notice how difficult these flames are to see. This painter chose a see-through pearl to give a subtle flame effect in certain light.

Black is the most difficult paint color to shoot. It shows every little flaw, scratch and paint swirl. Generally, only experienced paint and body men have success with dark colors. Pinstriping and flames have added greatly to the overall theme of this street rod.

Another look at how scallops give a retro look to older body styles.

Here is another look at a pearl paint job. Notice how the inside of the fender is blue and the outside is green. As you walk around the car, these tones change as your viewing angle changes.

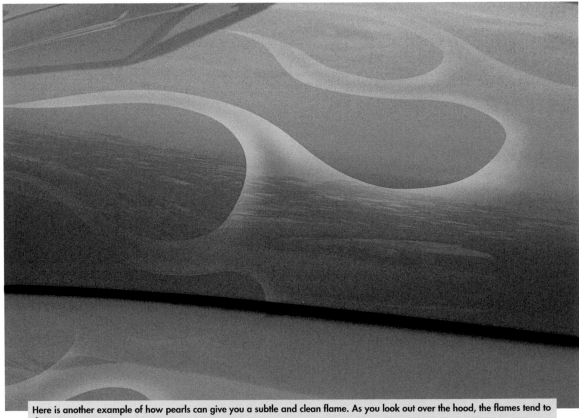

Here is another example of how pearls can give you a subtle and clean flame. As you look out over the hood, the flames tend to disappear.

Caricature details can either be purchased as decals or airbrushed by an artist. To pull this off, the Road Runner should be added to the engine compartment and interior as well.

Your painter can use your professional sketches to lay out graphics. This painter is laying out a series of flowing stripes that will mimic flames. Without a sketch, the painter or graphics artist will have to guess what you want, which is nearly impossible. *(Street Rods by Michael)*

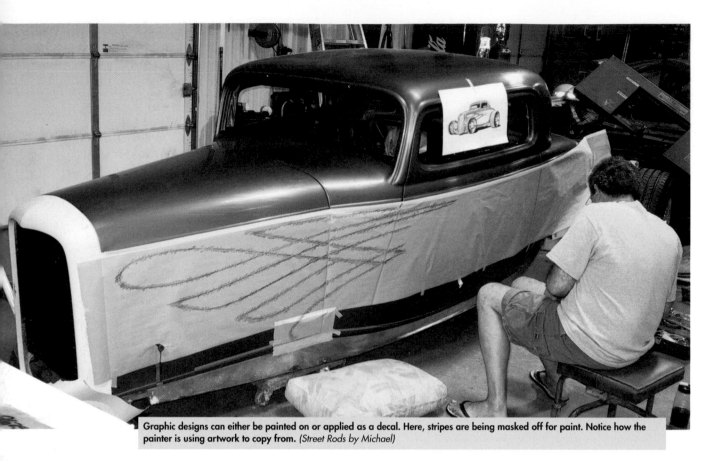

Graphic designs can either be painted on or applied as a decal. Here, stripes are being masked off for paint. Notice how the painter is using artwork to copy from. (Street Rods by Michael)

3-M offers transfer paper that can be used to match one design from one side of the car to the other. This paper allows you to trace your design and copy it ove to the other side. (Street Rods by Michael)

hours or less) and must have the clear coat applied wet-on-wet.

Clear coats and single-stage top coats are applied in much the same way. First, a half coat is applied to give the paint something to adhere to. Most painters call this a tack coat. After this coat has flashed off, a full coat can be applied. Repeat this process until a good three coats have been applied to the surface. Remember that these are wet, heavy coats so it will be easy to get runs. It is important to learn your paint brand's characteristics before painting any large areas. You may find that a 15-minute flash time is needed with some brands between every coat to avoid runs. Other brands will have the opposite problem in the sense that they may not run, but they are difficult to apply wet and glossy.

Experience will tell you if more coats are needed on the panels of the car. A few coats are removed during the color sanding and compounding process, so five to six coats may need to be applied to the exterior of the car or anything else you intend to polish. Urethane is a thick paint, unlike lacquer, so any talk you hear about applying 20 coats is left over from the lacquer days.

Solvent pop is a failure created by applying too much paint. Every paint is different, but three coats is a good average. You may need to spray the paint in heavier coats to get the paint to lay out the way

Most painters use fine line tape to draw out the actual design. This tape is offered by 3-M and is very flexible. It is also thin and helps prevent paint buildup near the tape edges. *(Street Rods by Michael)*

Pinstriping can be done before of after clearcoat, depending on the effect you are going for.
(Street Rods by Michael)

A view of the finished product almost perfectly matches the original artwork. *(Street Rods by Michael)*

you want it, in which case you may shoot two coats at a time. This requires trial and error to get right. You'll soon understand why good painters are hard to come by. Don't expect to paint like a professional right out of the gate. Painting chassis parts first will give you a chance to learn the characteristics of the paint before the large pieces are tackled.

You will need to experiment with your gun to understand how it sprays paint, but most painters spray with a full spraying pattern and hold the gun about 12 to 16 inches from the surface. Most paint companies offer a painting class to teach newcomers how to use their brand. A class like this is invaluable!

Special effects

Learning to paint flames, scallops and graphics requires additional skills that can take as much, or more, time as basic painting. Beginners should consider planning a simple paint scheme for their first project or enlist the help of a professional. If you want to learn, there are a few tricks that will help you get a more professional-looking finish.

Professionals spray the primary color and entire design in base coat first and then clear over the surface last. This greatly reduces the rough edges that tape lines can cause. 3M makes a blue fine-line tape that provides a finer edge than traditional masking tape.

For flames, the surface is first sprayed the primary color (usually black). Once the base coat has thoroughly dried for at least two hours, the flame pattern is taped off using 1/8-inch fine-line tape. The rest of the surface is masked off using paper and normal masking tape. The surface is repeatedly checked to see if any fine-line tape is lifting off and the flame area is tacked off before the flames are sprayed. It is important to keep the entire surface clean during the masking process because some base coats react with wax and grease remover. Although it's awkward at times, I like to wear rubber gloves when I'm masking to keep the oil on my skin from touching the car.

Many special effects, like scallops, are done on both sides of the car in mirror images. This is achieved by first drawing the pattern on two sheets of transfer paper and then laying the paper on the

Pinstriping can range from a simple highlight to an elaborate part of the theme. Experienced pinstripers often travel with the car shows, offering their services right on the spot.

surface. Transfer paper has a thin, sticky coat on the back that acts like tape and paper combined. I like to draw the image about 1/16-inch larger than desired and then run a thin border of fine-line tape over the exposed edges of the transfer paper. This seems to provide a little cleaner look than just transfer paper by itself.

Graphics are usually done by freehand with an airbrush. This skill is even beyond most professionals' ability and requires years of experience to perfect. Most people will first base coat the primary color and then take the car to an airbrush artist for any graphics work.

Runs and other problems

Problems with temperature, flash time, viscosity and coat thickness are the primary reasons for runs. Few paints set up well below 70 degrees. The lower the temperature, the longer the flash time. Some paints won't cure at all below 50 degrees. In cold weather, you may need to double the amount of time you wait before applying another coat. Professional painters use heated spray booths to speed cure times and create a good painting environment all year round. When a coat of primer, sealer, paint, etc., is applied, the surface will look wet. The time it takes for the reducer to flash off, or evaporate, is called flash time. If you put two wet coats on top of each other, you'll get runs, so allow each coat to flash off properly. A normal flash time is about 10 minutes at 75 degrees, with this time increasing/decreasing with the ambient air temperature.

Some painters mix their paint too thin in an effort to reduce orange peel. This technique works, but at the risk of runs. This essentially turns the paint into the same viscosity as lacquer, so the VOC content becomes higher than what was designed by the manufacturer. The main drawback to doing this is that your flash time increases, thereby exposing the surface to contaminants longer. You will also need twice as many coats, and the paint will "shrink" over time.

Just about any product that has a reducer added will shrink as it cures. What happens is that the surface dries, but reducer is still slowly evaporating out of the paint. This can be a problem if you have over-reduced all of your primer coats as well. It's frustrating when you finish your paint and go through the effort of color sanding and buffing the surface, only to have the surface look dull and pitted a month later. This happens when the products are over-reduced.

Fish eyes are caused when an oily contaminant is on the surface of the car before applying paint. When the paint hits this spot, it will push itself away from the contaminant and make a little circle that resembles a fish eye. This is a serious flaw and the entire surface will have to be wet sanded and resprayed. If this happens frequently, add an additional wax and grease remover step, use a different wax and grease remover, or try adding a small amount of fish eye eliminator liquid to the paint itself. Your paint supplier can help you find one that is compatible to your paint brand.

If sanding scratches can be seen in the paint after it has been polished, then you are not working your primer/surfacer up into finer grits of sand paper as you block. You will need to add additional sanding

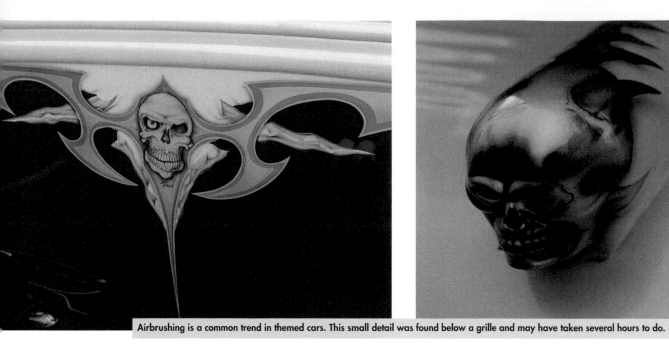

Airbrushing is a common trend in themed cars. This small detail was found below a grille and may have taken several hours to do.

Lighter paint colors are generally more forgiving for beginners to work with because they hide imperfections better than dark colors. If you intend to do all the bodywork yourself, going with a simple white base paint, like on this custom truck, can help you hide your places of "learning." *(Interiors By Shannon)*

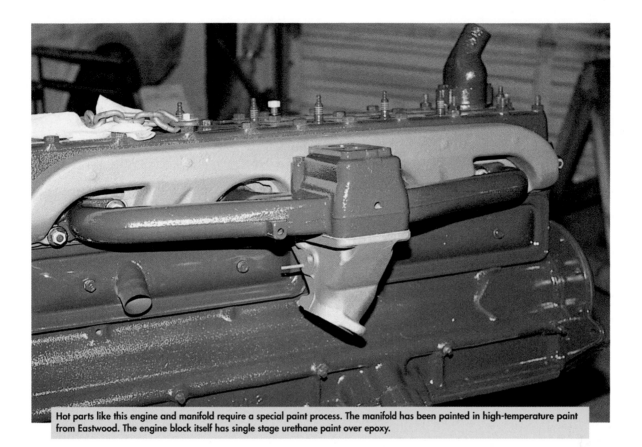

Hot parts like this engine and manifold require a special paint process. The manifold has been painted in high-temperature paint from Eastwood. The engine block itself has single stage urethane paint over epoxy.

steps to your process to cut the larger scratches down. It is easy to miss scratches if the surface does not have a guide coat to show you how much primer will need to be removed.

Hot parts

Parts that heat up need to be painted differently. Engine blocks and radiators should have one coat of epoxy primer and just enough paint to cover the primer. This is one place where the thinner the paint the better. If the engine pan or radiator has a dent you would like to repair, first tap the dent from the back side the best you can and then use J B Weld instead of traditional body filler. Once it's dry, the J B Weld can be sanded flush and reprimed with epoxy.

Whether or not you should use a base coat/clear coat system on these hot areas is debatable. I've seen several engine blocks shot in metallic paints with no problems. Some base coats don't withstand heat well, so ask your paint manufacturer if their base coats can be applied to engines. Neither of these paints will hold up on exhaust manifolds and are marginal on brake calipers. Special high-temperature paints can be purchased from Eastwood for the more extreme applications, like exhaust manifolds and systems.

As long as your bodywork has been done correctly, and you're clean and safe, you can be a good painter in time. This is one of those skills where practice makes perfect. Even the best painters make mistakes from time to time, so be patient if it doesn't come to you right away.

Chapter 11

Color Sanding and Polishing Paint

Wet sanding begins with 1,000-grit paper to break the surface. You can then move on to 1,500-grit to finish removing orange peel. A light sanding with 2,000-grit will make polishing easier.

URETHANE PAINTS ARE THE INDUSTRY STANDARD and can be polished just as fine as the old lacquers, but any bumpy surfaces, or orange peel, must be removed first. This process is called "color sanding." Color sanding is just a fancy term for wet sanding paint. There are many flaws or problems that can arise with paint, but three of them — small runs, dust specs and orange peel — can be repaired in the color sanding process.

All three flaws can be repaired, but the runs are the most serious and difficult to fix. A run will form whenever more paint is applied to a surface than it can hold. Applying thick coats, poor spraying or coverage technique, cold temperature, improper gun setup and over-reduced paint can all cause runs. However, overcompensation can create dry or orange-peeled paint, so there is a balance that must be achieved. Some paints lay out flatter than others. Some are easy to run. Others are almost impossible to run, but dry with severe orange peel. Every painter has a different preference.

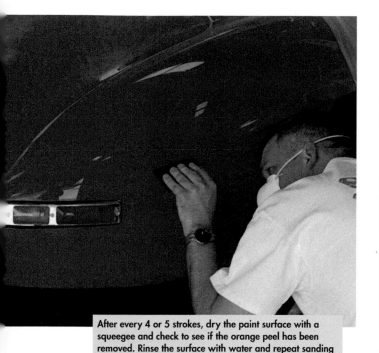

After every 4 or 5 strokes, dry the paint surface with a squeegee and check to see if the orange peel has been removed. Rinse the surface with water and repeat sanding if necessary.

Repairing runs

Some runs can be repaired before the color sanding process. Many painters will take a new razor blade and scratch the run off once the paint has fully cured. This is done by laying the blade on top of the run, perpendicular to the surface, and lightly scratching back and forth in the direction of the run. The run will begin to look dull as the layers are scratched off. Great care must be given to avoid scratching the paint on either side of the run as the paint is not very thick there.

One trick that will help is to take a small grinder and file the sharp corners off each end of the blade. This should help reduce damaging scratches that can be caused by the sharp 90-degree edge of the razor blade. As you continue to lightly scrape away at the run, the dull, scratched area gets wider. This scratching process should be repeated until all of the run has been removed and the spot is flush with the surrounding area. Then continue with the normal color sanding process. This technique will not work 100 percent of the time and takes some practice, but it can save a lot of time once it's perfected.

Color sanding

Before any sanding or polishing, you need to mask off the car just as you would during the paint process. Polishing is very messy and can create a cleanup nightmare. The paper will keep excess compound and paint out of important areas.

Color sanding removes the minor flaws of dust particles and orange peel in the paint. Urethane paints have a curing time that's based on heat, and they get harder as the curing process develops. Professional painters have spray booths that heat the paint to more than 150 degrees. At this temperature, urethane paint takes less than an hour to set up. If you lightly press your fingernail to the surfaces of the paint and it leaves a mark, then the paint has not cured enough for color sanding. However, if you wait

When you are color sanding and polishing, make sure the surface is free of all grit and dirt. Constantly wash the surface and check for grit with your hands.

Buffing pads pick up dirt and dust from the air. Store them in a plastic bag or container when they are not being used. Wool pads should be cleaned with a spur before polishing and foam pads can be hand washed.

too long, the paint will get so hard that the polishing process becomes difficult. You want to be polishing as soon as the paint has cured. Twenty-four hours seems to be a good rule of thumb in warm weather.

You must have a clean surface to color sand and polish paint. The smallest piece of grit can get trapped between the sandpaper and paint. This can cause damaging scratches. Wash the surface off before any work begins.

3M has a 6-inch wet-sanding block that is perfect for color sanding. Using a block and 1,000-grit wet sandpaper, lightly sand the surface of the paint. Sand only a few strokes and then dry the surface with a rubber squeegee. Look at the light reflection on the surface carefully. You should see just the tops of the orange peel sanded and turning dull. The low spots of the orange peel are untouched and shiny looking.

Color sanding is done in small sections at a time, approximately 6 by 6-inch areas. Rinse water over the area and repeat the process until the shiny low spots get noticeably smaller but do not disappear. You then switch to a 1,500-grit paper and continue to color sand until all of the low, shiny spots have disappeared. Lightly color sand the area again with 2,000-grit before any polishing begins. Most painters finish an entire section, meaning body, hood,

Apply a line of compound around the pad and spread around the surface of the paint before spinning the motor. Excess compound will just sling off and be wasted.

fenders, etc. with one grit at a time. Don't be alarmed if it seems you are using a lot of sandpaper. This is normal. Urethane is hard on sandpaper. You may go through 30 sheets or more.

Obviously, this process takes a lot of time, so many painters will opt to paint cars in sections. For example, they paint and polish the body first and then move on to the fenders. This way you always work with fresh paint, which is softer and easier to use.

Polishing

Polishing should be done in stages, much like color sanding. There are different grits of polishing compound to match the hardness of the paint. I use a fairly soft paint, so I begin the polishing process with 3M Finesse-it II, which has no abrasive grit, and a wool buffing pad. Other paints may require some abrasive like 3M Imperial compound to start out with, so do not hesitate to call your paint supplier and get recommendations.

It is easy to "burn" an edge when you are buffing paint. This means that you buffed all the paint off a metal edge. It can happen quickly if you are not careful. When you buff paint, always be conscious

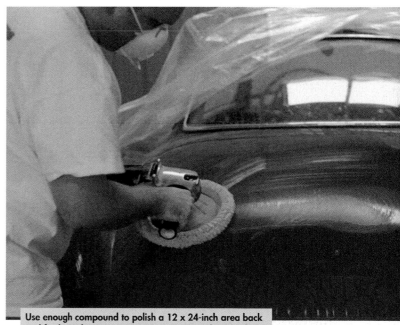

Use enough compound to polish a 12 x 24-inch area back and forth. Make sure not to stay in any one place too long or you will burn the paint.

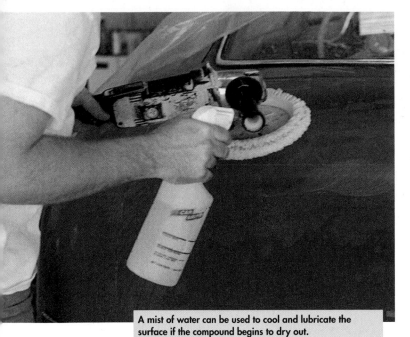

A mist of water can be used to cool and lubricate the surface if the compound begins to dry out.

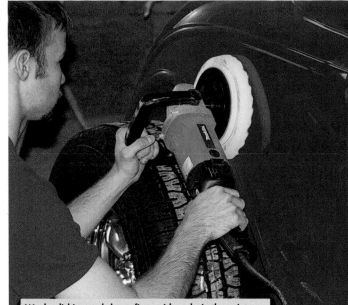

Wool polishing pads leave fine swirl marks in the paint. Foam polishing pads and special compound are used to remove these.

The foam polishing technique is the same as using the wool pad. Be sure to watch the direction that the pad is traveling. Always polish off an edge and cover sharp edges like drip rails with masking tape for protection.

of the direction the pad is traveling. Sharp edges that the pad will come in contact with, like drip rails, should be covered with several layers of tape to prevent a burn-through. When you approach edges, make sure the pad is swirling off the edge and never into one. If your pad is not polishing the paint, don't compensate by pressing down on the paint harder, just switch to a compound that has some abrasive in it. It is important to always keep the surface of the paint lubricated so you do not overheat the pad and damage the paint. You can prevent this by moving your pad around the entire section and buff in stages. Do not try to bring a small spot to a high luster in one pass. Keep plenty of compound on the surface and occasionally mist the surface with water to keep the area wet and cool.

On sunny days, you may have noticed that many dark-colored cars have swirl marks in the paint. These are very fine scratches that are usually caused by the owner during the cleaning and waxing process. The slightest dust particle trapped between the paint and rag can cause these. The wool polishing pads leave the same marks, so another process is needed to

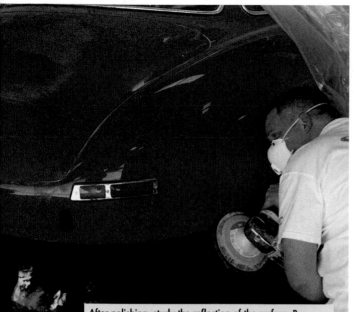

After polishing, study the reflection of the surface. By moving your head from left to right, you will be able to pick up slight imperfections such as sanding scratches or missed orange peel in the reflection. Show cars are void of any such imperfections. Expect to pay $1,500 to $3,500 for color sanding and polishing in most shops, depending on the size of the vehicle and depth of detail you are seeking.

You can see the difference between this fender and the trunk lid. The trunk lid is not reflecting the ceiling lights like the top of the fender. You can read newspaper print in the reflection of a show car, but this may not be practical for most custom cars.

remove the swirl marks. 3M makes a foam polishing pad and polish just for this purpose. The surface needs to be free of other polishing compounds or dust, but the technique is the same used with wool pads. Some compounds have a chemical that can eventually damage the paint so be sure to remove any excess compound as soon as you are finished.

Nib files are mounted on blocks of wood and can be a great help in fixing imperfections in the paint before color sanding and polishing begins. (Eastwood Company)

Chapter 12

Wiring

THE WIRING FOR YOUR CAR SHOULD BE DONE before the car is sent off for upholstery. At this point, your car has been painted and you are over the hump! Extra care must now be given to ensure the finish does not get scratched. New paint jobs should breathe, so it is not a good idea to use a car cover or place anything on the vehicle for several months. Often, this will leave an impression or indentation on new paint. Ultimately, you just have to be careful.

Rules:

1. Never store anything near the car that can fall on it.
2. Never set anything on the surface of the car, like a tool.
3. Never wear jewelry or a belt when working on your car.

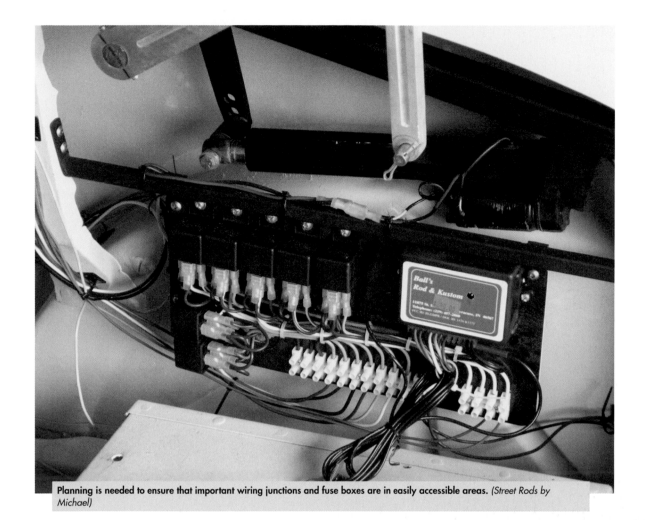

Planning is needed to ensure that important wiring junctions and fuse boxes are in easily accessible areas. (*Street Rods by Michael*)

Belt buckles and tools are the number one reason for damaged paint.

Wiring a car intimidates a lot of people because they think you have to go down to Radio Shack, buy a spool of wire and build the harness from scratch. It can be done this way, but the sound of it intimidates me, too. There is a much easier way. A complete wiring kit can be purchased from Affordable Street Rods or other harness companies for around $300.

The basic idea for automotive wiring is that the power comes off the battery through an ignition switch to the starter and power panel. The power panel (fuse panel) distributes the power to each individual circuit with a fuse for safety reasons.

Now, I've seen some rodders bypass the fuses to save time. Let's just say I unsuccessfully tried this very thing when I was in high school. Some months afterwards a short in the radio triggered a domino effect that rapidly set all of my wires in the car on fire. This normally would be enough to ruin your day, except this event happened at the exact same time I was being pulled over for a minor traffic violation. Well, the fire department showed up, and then my

Here is another example of how wiring can affect your interior planning. Stereo equipment and wiring both need to be integrated into the design.

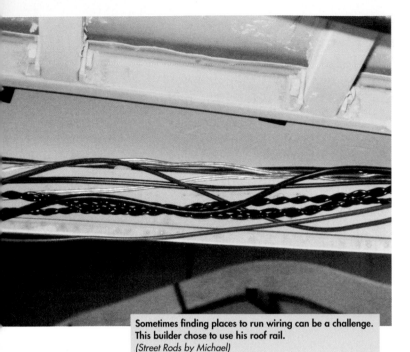

Sometimes finding places to run wiring can be a challenge. This builder chose to use his roof rail. *(Street Rods by Michael)*

As you can see, the space under the dash is somewhat limited, so you should wire your car before installing the dash. *(Street Rods by Michael)*

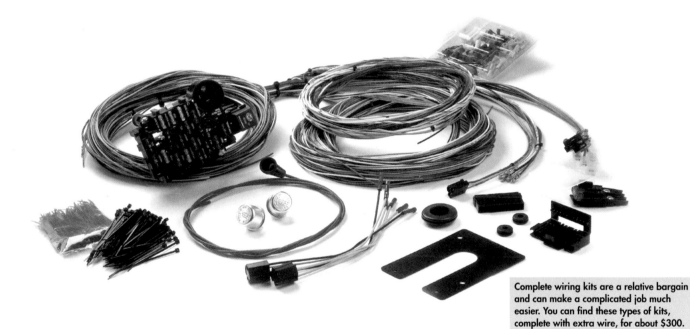

Complete wiring kits are a relative bargain and can make a complicated job much easier. You can find these types of kits, complete with extra wire, for about $300. *(Easton Company)*

parents. It wasn't exactly my finest hour, but at least I learned some of my lessons early! Trust me, the fuses are there for a reason.

The nice thing about a kit is that the fuse box and wires are labeled so all you have to do is run the wires to a location and hook them up to the appropriate number on the fuse box. It's pretty easy. When you order your kit, the company will need to know what type of engine you have, whether it is fuel injected and how many power-operated accessories, such as power seats or windows, that you have.

Some kits are manufactured without the connections attached. These kits usually have extra wire with the connectors provided in a bag. These kits are useful for non-standard applications like custom cars. If you receive a kit like this, you will have to cut the wire to length and solder the connection yourself. This isn't really that much work. I prefer this type of kit because the other types will often be short in places and require modification anyway. In any case, make sure all the connections are soldered and not just crimped into place.

Chapter 13

Interiors

THERE IS A LOT OF WORK ON CUSTOM CARS that owners can do themselves, but when it comes to upholstery, there are limitations. Many models have interior kits available for as little as $500. These kits provide an OEM-style interior that you can install yourself with a minimal tool investment. The door, trunk and kick panels either snap or screw into place. The carpet can be glued down using a 3M 8080 spray glue, and the seat covers slip over the old padding and hog ring in place.

Sure, the price is right, but these kits are all OEM, which kind of defeats the purpose in a custom car. To get custom work, you will have to take your car to an upholstery shop. There are custom interior specialists all over the country and prices start around $3,500 and can go over $10,000, depending on how elaborate you want to get. The average upholstery job costs around $5,000.

We'll use a shop in Alexander City, Alabama, to understand the interior process better. Shannon Walters, owner of Interiors by Shannon, has been working with custom upholstery for years and has several tips to simplify planning and reduce cost.

The basics

Upholstery begins with the wind lace and headliner installation. Most cars use some kind of cloth headliner to reduce cost, but many different

If the outside of the car is lightly modified, then original items like the dash cluster can create balance and save money. *(Interiors By Shannon)*

Billet aluminum is very popular in custom interiors. Just about any design can be cut from aluminum block, which gives builders infinite possibilities. *(Interiors By Shannon)*

Most interior designs have to be thought out in advance. Gauges have to be selected and laid out well before the paint process. *(Interiors By Shannon)*

materials can be used. Most of the seat fittings and consoles are manufactured before the carpet is installed. This is done mostly just to keep the carpet clean. There's no need to walk on the carpet and possibly damage it while the interior is in a construction phase.

Carpet is found in two primary materials: wool and nylon. Wool is frequently used in show cars, but the extra expense is not necessary for most custom cars.

Master cylinder

Some hot rods have master cylinders mounted

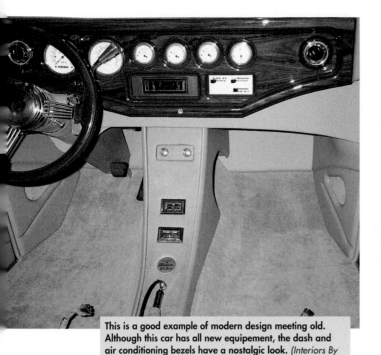
This is a good example of modern design meeting old. Although this car has all new equipement, the dash and air conditioning bezels have a nostalgic look. *(Interiors By Shannon)*

Although this dash appears to have no instrumentation, all the gauges are digital within the narrow center strip.

under the floor so you have two options to add brake fluid—you can cut a hole in your carpet to give you a flip-up tab, or install a remote filler tube to give you access in the engine compartment. If you go with the first option, it is only a matter of time before you stain the carpet. Remote filler tubes and master cylinders add about $200 and can be worth every penny. Most models have a door sill plate that covers the edge of the carpet along the door openings. The upholsterer will need these to install the carpet. Many styles can be purchased from Valley Auto Accessories and other companies.

Dash

When designing a custom dash, be aware that the dash cannot rest flush against the door. Many vehicles have 1/2-inch-thick wind lacing around the door that lies between the A pillar and the dash. The door panels are 3/4-inch thick as well and could be more.

Dashes can be painted or covered in material. OEM dashes were painted all the way through the 1950s and seem to still be very popular at the shows. SEM makes an aerosol paint for vinyl which works well on metal, too. It matches both the color and gloss of leather and is ideal for seat frames, garnish moldings and dashes.

Wiring tips

Interior design and electrical wiring work

Not all dashes have to be painting. This one has been covered with suede to match the rest of the interior.

together much like the body and chassis do. One is dependant on the other. An interior design must be sketched out before any wiring can take place. For example, will your car have power windows and if so, where will the switches be? Where will the speakers be mounted? Will you run your stereo up to a console in the ceiling, dash, floor or trunk? This all needs to be planned out. Then the vehicle wiring must be

This modern roadster has a nod to nostalgia with low-back seats and simple instrumentation. *(Interiors By Shannon)*

Make sure your dash is completely wired and finished before sending the car to the interior shop. It is also a good idea to run the engine and test the gauges while everything is easy to get to. *(Interiors By Shannon)*

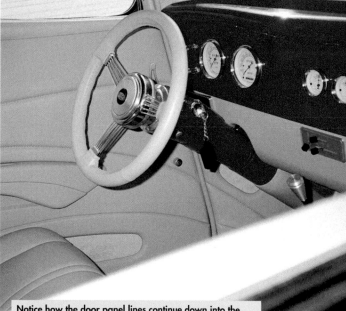

Notice how the door panel lines continue down into the kick panel. Added details like this don't add much to the cost. *(Interiors By Shannon)*

finished before the interior can begin.

Shannon Walters recommends that you leave slack in all of your wires just in case the upholstery shop needs to make adjustments. This is easily done by using plastic ties and running loops near the end of each wire. Allow 4 inches of play just in case, and be sure to leave slack in the entire wiring harness. There is no advantage to running your wires tight. If you are concerned about them moving around, then use plastic ties every foot or so to hold the wiring

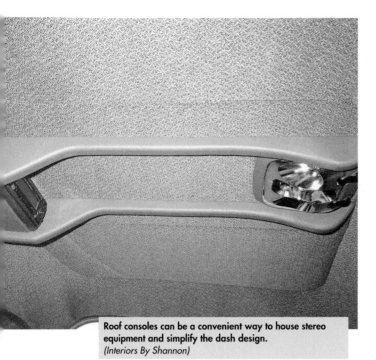

Roof consoles can be a convenient way to house stereo equipment and simplify the dash design.
(Interiors By Shannon)

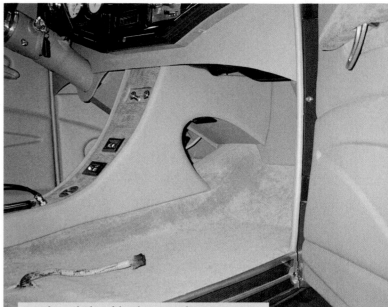

Consoles are both useful and attractive, but require planning when it comes to wiring. The cord coming out the carpet in this car is for the power seats.
(Interiors By Shannon)

harness in place.

The small panel down by your feet between the door and the firewall is called the kick panel. There needs to be enough slack so the wires can travel from the dash up over these panels and out to the doors. Your heater hoses should have slack in them for the same reason. Many people like to run these under the dash, to the kick panels and out through the inner fender well area to avoid cutting any holes in the firewall. This is for aesthetic reasons only, but if you do this, install a metal spring in the hose where sharp bends occur to keep the hose from collapsing.

Insulation

Be sure to put insulation in your car before taking it to the upholsterer. Insulation can be purchased from places like Yogi's Inc. and is easy to install. The insulation comes in stock sheets about 1/4-inch thick and can be cut to fit all of the flat surfaces inside the car. The door skins, firewall, floor, trunk, etc. are all prime candidates for this treatment.

Insulation makes a significant difference in a car's interior. Not only is road noise reduced, but vibration and little squeaks seem to disappear as well. The whole quality of the ride improves.

Seats

There are a couple of factors to consider when installing seats. As far as planning goes, seatbacks without headrests should not rise higher than the bottom of the door window. In other words, if you are looking at the outside of the car, you should not see the seats above the window edge, and double check to see that the seatbacks are the same height. This is for aesthetics more than functionality. The seats need to be mounted level and square to the car. Special care needs to be given to bucket seats to make sure the tracks are in the same place on either side of the car. When mounting old seats, make sure you compensate for worn or missing cushion material. New foam will be about an inch higher than the exposed seat frame. This new foam will also be on the sides of the seat, so factor this in so the seats do not rub on the door panels. If you are using old seat frames, save some money and remove all of the old material. There is no reason to pay somebody else to do that.

Windows

All of the windows need to be installed, adjusted and working before the upholsterer can finish the job. Have you ever seen the brown bubbles that form on the edges of old automotive glass? There is a chemical in some window adhesives that attacks the plastic in laminated glass. Walters has a tip to prevent this: Put a thin coat of aquarium sealant around the edge of the glass before you put it in the frame. This will keep the window adhesive from touching the lamination. Aquarium sealants have silicon in them, so make sure you use them sparingly and away from any areas where painting is done. The window felting needs to be installed and the garnish moldings painted and fitted ahead of time.

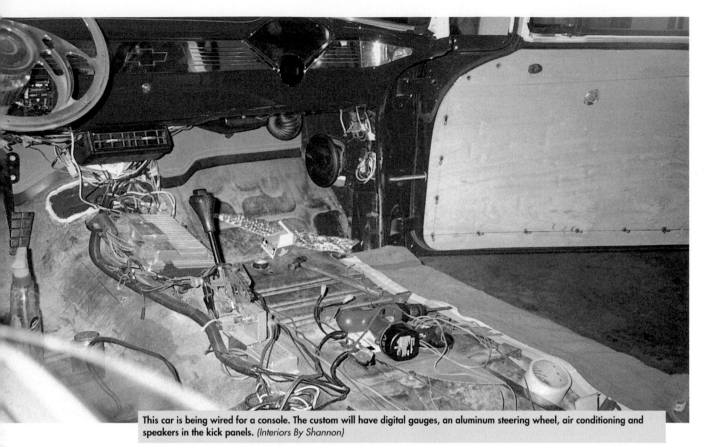

This car is being wired for a console. The custom will have digital gauges, an aluminum steering wheel, air conditioning and speakers in the kick panels. (Interiors By Shannon)

Bucket seats are an easy way to create luxury and comfort in your ride. They generally ride better than bench seats. (Interiors By Shannon)

When going without headrests, it is a good idea to keep the seat backs flush with the top of the door. This gives an overall clean, sharp appearance. (Interiors By Shannon)

Upholstery styles

Once you get to the upholsterer, there are some basic choices involved in the styling of the interior. The first choice is the kind of material you will use. Cloth is the least expensive of the materials and has the widest selection of patterns and colors. In custom cars, tweed is used frequently and is ideal for headliners, doors, etc. Tweed is a little harder to clean, so you may want to consider something smooth like vinyl or panel board on areas your feet touch, like kick panels.

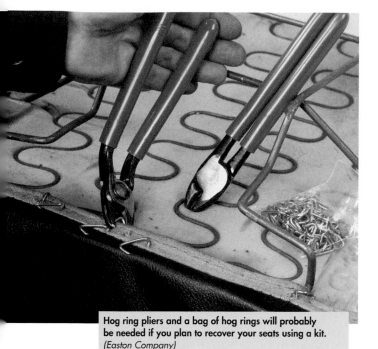

Hog ring pliers and a bag of hog rings will probably be needed if you plan to recover your seats using a kit. (Easton Company)

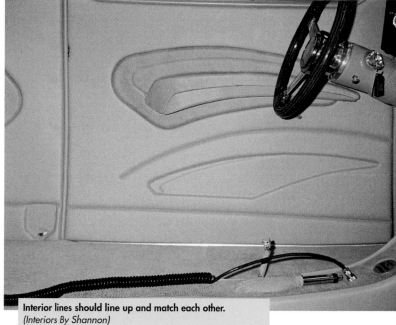

Interior lines should line up and match each other. (Interiors By Shannon)

You do not see too much cloth in trunk areas, mainly because the trunk is rarely seen, but show cars are expected to have this area finished to the same detail as the rest of the car, and this usually means leather. Most people carry the interior theme to the trunk, but this is an easy place to cut back in order to meet budgets. Trunk mats and panel board are nice, affordable replacements.

Vinyl became popular in the 1950s as an inexpensive way to simulate leather. The old sales brochures are fun to read because vinyl was given all kinds of names that sound like animal hide: leatherette, morokide or Naugahyde. Vinyl has some practical uses, too. It resists water damage, which makes it ideal for convertibles and boats.

However, the cost of leather has been coming down and now adds about $1,000 to the total cost. It's important to be happy with your interior. You see the interior every time you get in the car, but rarely crawl underneath, so it seems to make sense to put the money where it will be most appreciated. Why spend $1,000 extra for an assortment of chrome or polished chassis parts under the car and then cut back on what is highly visible?

Decoration within the material itself is done several ways. Patterns can be sewn in the material with thread to visually break up large areas. Pleats are used the same way, but usually have to be used in straight lines. Buttons, beads and rhinestones have all been used, but are very uncommon in street rods. The factory would often mix colored fabrics and stitch them together. Most of the 1950s cars were done this way, where the border of the seat would be the primary color and an insert was stitched in

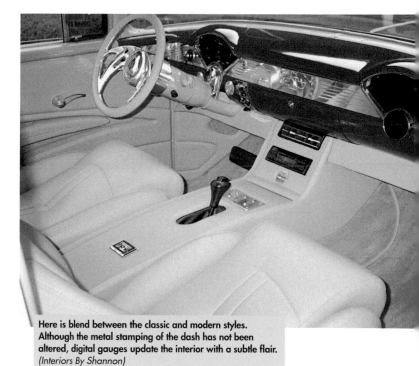

Here is blend between the classic and modern styles. Although the metal stamping of the dash has not been altered, digital gauges update the interior with a subtle flair. (Interiors By Shannon)

to give contrast. This is still very popular on custom cars today and is done with all materials.

Different stitching can be used to add detail, too. Top stitching is the technique used to sew patterns or designs into the material. Different-colored thread can add to the effect because the thread is visible. The stitch is not used to join two pieces of material, it is only used for decoration. A plain stitch is used to join material, and the thread is not visible, as it is under the material. Plain stitching is used to create patterns similar to top stitching, but is much more

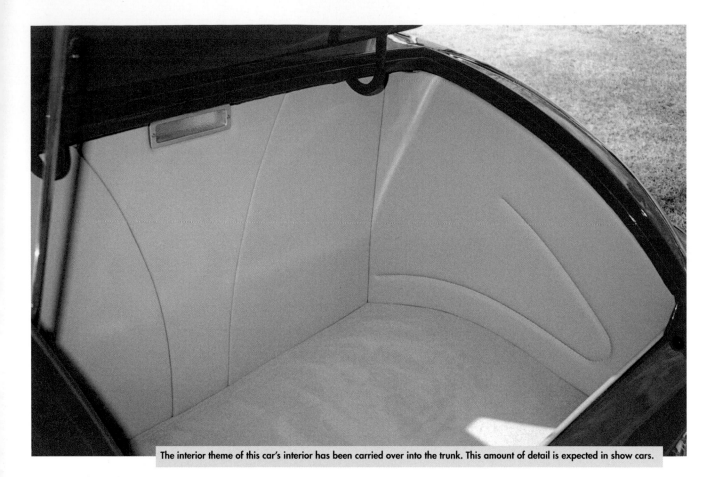

The interior theme of this car's interior has been carried over into the trunk. This amount of detail is expected in show cars.

How many colors do you want to incorporate into your interior theme? There is a balance between monochromatic and multi-colored patterns. Some colors work better than others. For example, I saw a beautiful car at a show with a red theme. Everything was red inside and out. Although the workmanship was outstanding, the details were hidden because everything was the same color.

time consuming for the upholsterer. Instead of using one piece, the upholsterer must measure and cut smaller pieces and join them together so they appear to be one piece. This is very popular in custom cars. Welt cord was used in the seams at the factory, but seems to have fallen out of favor in the customizing world. You may want to use it if you are seeking a nostalgic look. French seams are very popular and have stitched thread on either side of the seam, much like a baseball. Small logos and personalized designs are done with embroidery. It's common to see car logos like the Chevy bowtie stitched into the seats as an accent.

You pay for detail in upholstery much the way you do with paint. Obviously, the more elaborate the design, the more it will cost. As with paint, it is a good idea to get a reference or see the quality of the shop's work before you begin. An interior package usually takes four to six weeks to complete. Always check the shop's availability several months in advance and ask to be put on their schedule. The better shops will have months of work lined up at any given time.

Chapter 14

Restoring Trim

THE DECISION ON WHETHER TO RESTORE TRIM and the planning of an overall theme go hand in hand. Trim generally includes bumpers, lenses, OEM emblems, stainless moldings, hood ornaments, etc. Try to design a theme that is consistent. Are you building a modern "high-tech" look or going with a nostalgic one? Putting in digital gauges, removing the bumpers and keeping the OEM stainless moldings will appear out of balance. Designing the trim layout up front is critical to the overall success of the project.

Chrome continues to get more expensive every year. I've worked on cars that had $20,000 in chrome work alone. Any car from the '50s will be covered in an assortment of chrome and stainless. All of these ornament and molding locations have holes drilled into the steel. The holes will need to be welded up if

This is an example of how money can be saved with limited trim. Side moldings don't have to be restored and neither do the bumpers.

The small amount of trim that was used here was all custom manufactured, which can be time consuming and very expensive.

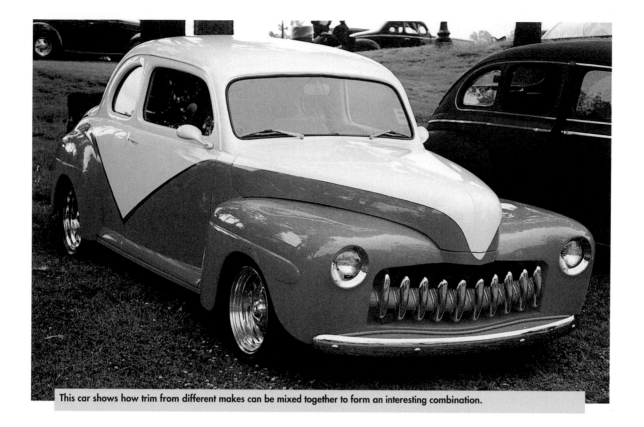

This car shows how trim from different makes can be mixed together to form an interesting combination.

you intend to delete the trim, so if you wait until after the car is painted to make a decision, it's too late.

Many hot rodders eliminate all the OEM trim and create their own. All kinds of creative parts can be cut out of stainless stock and polished to look OEM. Most winning show cars incorporate custom-made trim. It's the only way to really ensure that you have a "one-of-a-kind" appearance.

If you are trying to keep a budget under control or reduce expenses, then go with a clean, stripped-down look. Many custom car builders use the monochromatic look successfully. You may choose to remove all of the trim and weld up the holes or paint all of the trim body color. You could have a metallic emerald green body and paint the trim a darker shade of green and come out with a gorgeous car. Paint the trim bright yellow and you may have a different story, but there is a lot of room for artistic expression.

If you stay with chrome, it will have to be sent to a professional, but you can save money by doing other trim restoration yourself. For example, aluminum parts can be bought polished or unpolished. Valve covers, headers, intake manifolds, etc. could all be polished by the builder himself. Buffing kits complete with motor, wheels and compounds can be purchased for around $500.

The theory behind polishing metal is the same as polishing paint: You work your part in stages using different wheels and compounds until the desired luster is achieved. Different metals require different compounds depending on how hard the metal is. Kits come with instructions explaining which compound and technique to use for a given metal.

The trim running down the side of many vehicles is perhaps the most difficult to restore because it is thin and usually dented. Up until the 1960s, this trim was almost always made out of stainless steel. Stainless is about as hard a metal as you can find on a car, but it can be restored. If the metal has large dents or has been crushed, it is probably beyond repair, so check to see if the part is being reproduced. If not, you will need to find a replacement from a salvage yard. However, scratches, chips and dime-size dents can all be repaired.

Dents need to be addressed first. A small body hammer and anvil are used to tap the dent from the inside out. This tapping process should be done a little at a time until the dent becomes flush with the anvil. When you feel the dent has been worked out, inspect the trim by running your fingers over the dent. You should feel dozens of tiny high and low spots where the dent has been worked out. If the whole area feels high or raised up, that is an indication

If you choose to keep all the original trim in a car like this, be prepared to spend upwards of $10,000 to get everything restored.

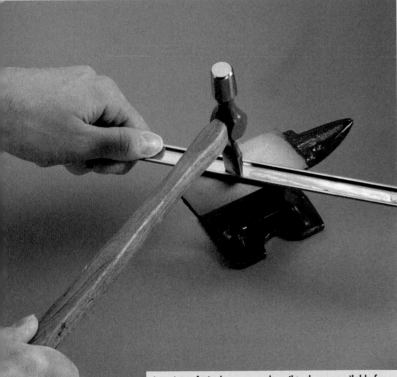

A variety of trim hammer and anvil tools are available for salvaging and straightening chrome. *(Eastwood Company)*

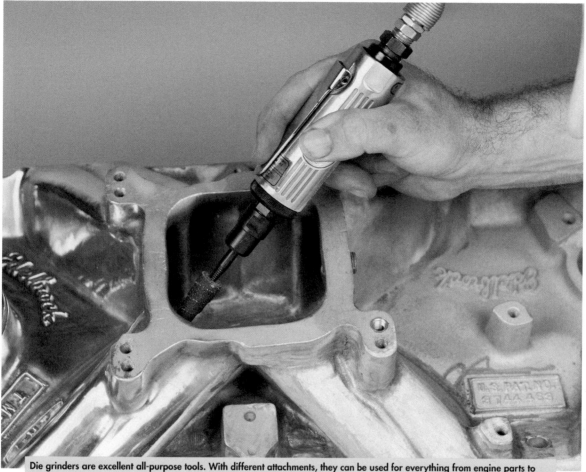

Die grinders are excellent all-purpose tools. With different attachments, they can be used for everything from engine parts to trim. *(Eastwood Company)*

that you have been tapping too hard or haven't kept the trim flush against the anvil. You can check your work by sanding the outside of the steel with a dual-action sander and 320-grit paper. The high spots will scratch first, leaving the low spots untouched. The differences between the two should be very slight and you may need to work some areas again. Then sand the area so all high and low spots have been removed. You literally cut the surface down so the whole area is flush with the lowest point. This should tell you that the difference between the high and low spots can be no greater than the thickness of the steel itself or you will end up with holes in the metal. This technique takes practice but ultimately isn't difficult to perfect. The 320-grit paper will remove the scratches and small nicks, too.

The 320-grit scratches then have to be removed. Most dual-action sanders have a locking mechanism that converts them to grinders. Use 400-grit paper and a grinder to lightly work over all of the 320 scratches. The 400-grit is aggressive and will get the steel so hot that it can turn blue, so constantly move the grinder around the surface to disperse the heat. Stop as soon as the circular scratches are gone.

Repeat the process with 600- and 800-grit paper. The 800-grit is so smooth that the surface will almost look polished. You can inspect the surface once again to see if you're satisfied with the finish. Sometimes you will see wavy or distorted areas near the dent and these can be worked out again, but try to decide how far you want to go.

It takes countless hours of tapping to get stainless "perfect." When you are satisfied that the scratches and dents are removed, you can finish polishing the steel with the stainless compounds provided in the buffing kit.

Chapter 15

Wrapping Up

If you are going to have a lot of chrome work done, make sure to allow plenty of time (and money) for the process to get done right.

THERE IS A SAYING BY PEOPLE WHO BUILD CARS that the last 5 percent of a car build takes 95 percent of the time. This is an exaggeration, but you will understand what they mean when you get to this stage. Part of the problem is psychological—once the car has been painted, a certain excitement and impatience builds up. Everything seems to take longer.

It is during this step when you find out that parts are missing and which components don't line up. In other words, you find out that your plan had holes in it.

Chrome plating and hardware

It's a good idea to get a jump on a couple of things before you get to the final stage. Chrome plating is one of them. Chrome is both time consuming and expensive (refer to Chapter 2). If you are concerned about cost, try to cut back on the chrome as possible. New environmental laws have increased the expense some, but the majority of the cost is labor. Each part is plated in copper and that metal is actually used like primer. The copper is sanded and buffed until the

Above, a batch of parts has just come in from the plate shop. These have a clear cadmium finish, which looks like a frosted silver. Cadmium is what most manufacturers used through the 1970s.

Professionals use a sandblasting cabinet like this one to strip small parts. Most hardware platers will offer this service along with the plating for a fee. If you like to strip the parts yourself, a tool like this can be purchased for around $300. (Eastwood Company)

imperfections of the part are removed. The process is time consuming and can take several months, so send the chrome out around the same time you are doing bodywork.

Your hardware, nuts and bolts can be plated in a variety of finishes. These parts will have to be purchased if you have a fiberglass kit, but many of these pieces can be saved when working with original bodies. Most original parts were plated in a cadmium finish. Today, manufacturers use a clear zinc finish. Both are silver metalic in color. If you like, you can get parts plated in a few other colors like gold, black and blue-green. There are companies that specialize in this form of plating and can even bead-blast all of the rust off for you.

Paint and powder coating your hardware is also an option, but you will need to make sure that the paint stays off the threads. This finish is not practical, however, as you run the risk of chipping during assembly. One tip to assist you here is to wrap the bolt head in masking tape to protect its finish from the wrench. These parts cannot be torqued to the same degree as plated parts.

Most rodders think of chrome plating when they think of hardware, but you have many other choices. I like to use chrome only in the highly exposed areas like the dash and engine compartment. You can save money in just about any other application.

Assembly and shimming

When installing components on your vehicle,

Tape is used to protect the paint around this radio antenna mount. Once the test fitting has been completed, the tape can be removed and the antenna mounted for the final time. Precautions like this can save countless hours of work.

protect painted surfaces with foam padding or masking tape. Installing hoods and trunk lids are two of the trickiest jobs. Some makes are pretty heavy and it is easy to scratch fenders and body areas during installation. A layer of padding can protect countless hours of work. All heavy parts should be

The key to good trim installation is to do it only once. Start with the back and move forward. The rear has the least amount of adjustment. As you move forward, make adjustments as necessary to get a straight, continuous flow. If you tighten down and dent the paint, you are tightening too hard.

handled by two people. Never try to line up big parts by yourself.

If the panels do not line up properly, remember that shims can be used to help. For example, if the gap between the door jam and the top of the door is too tight, add a shim between the frame and body. Most of the body bolts will have to be loosened and the body slightly lifted to accomplish this. The shim will have to be inserted near the door jam. When tightned, the shim slightly bends the body so the gap at the top of the door increases. If you have had the opposite problem, with a large gap at the top of the door, then shims can be added at the rear of the car and at the firewall to warp the body the other way. Some trial and error is needed to get shimming right. All you need is patience.

When using a wrench or ratchet near painted surfaces, hold the wrench with both hands and use one hand to cover the end of the tool. This technique will help keep the end of the tool from striking a painted surface during assembly.

As is the case when assembling fiberglass, do not overtighten components that bolt to a painted surface. Nylon lock nuts should also be used to fasten stainless moldings, emblems, chrome, etc. If the part begins to make an impression into the paint, then you are tightening too hard. Lock nuts and washers keep the part on, not force.

Glass

Most hot rods have flat glass all the way around the car. This greatly simplifies glass installation. Most flat glass can be purchased and cut locally. In the late 1940s and 1950s, auto manufacturers introduced curved glass, which presents a problem if your top is chopped. The curved glass will have to be trimmed to fit the new windshield frame. A good source for automotive glass is City Glass & Upholstery in Tacoma, Washington, which may have cut glass already.

In a pinch, I've cut curved glass myself using a diamond-coated cutoff disc and a Dremel tool. As long as you cut very slowly and keep a stream of water running over the glass, you should be successful.

Make sure replacement glass can be purchased if you decide to do it yourself and make a mistake. Like steel, you can always cut more off if you need to, so be conservative with your measurements.

The glass installation process takes some practice. Most medium to large cities have a glass installation service. They mostly serve the collision repair industry. Windshield installation can be so

If you are having trouble removing your steering wheel, you may need a steering wheel remover. This tool pops them right off. *(Eastwood Company)*

Most door handles have a retention spring or screw that holds them in place. These handles require a special tool to install and remove them. *(Eastwood Company)*

frustrating that I recommend using one of these services if possible. They are usually reasonably priced.

Door glass can be heavy, so line the doors slightly too high to compensate for the weight of the window mechanism and glass. It is a good idea to have all of this work done before upholstery.

Have the right tools

Knowing when to use the right tool is key. Certain parts can only be removed or installed with specialized tools. Steering wheels, bearings, bezels and moldings are perfect examples. Never try to force a part on or off a car and risk damaging it. It may just need a different tool. Power tools are great time savers during the disassembly phase of a car, but once everything has been painted it is a good idea to slow down. Hand tools provide much more control and reduce the risk of damaging paint. Perhaps more mistakes are made by professionals trying to rush a car for a show than any other reason. Try not to force the situation. Take your time and do things right. There will always be another show.

Odds and ends

There will be all kinds of little odds and ends to order, like gauges, accessories and weather stripping. The Internet is obviously a good place to network from. Sites like www.hotrodhotline.com and www.hotrodsuperstore are great places to start. There is also a huge listing of suppliers at the back of this book. Most companies don't mind if you call them and ask for help. If you get stuck trying to find a part, pick up the phone and start calling companies. Chances are if they don't have it, they can recommend somebody who does. The key is to develop a project plan that delivers parts when you need them.

Chapter 16

Care and Maintenance

Most of the time, you can keep your car reasonably clean with just a dust mop. They are easy to use, don't scratch the paint, and can be machine washed. *(Eastwood Company)*

ONCE THE CAR IS FINISHED, you'll probably ask yourself the question, "What do I do next?" Building a car takes countless hours and great perseverance. Many people immediately start new projects because for them the fun is in the build process. I must admit that I fall into that group, but there are a few things you should think about before you move on to your next car.

Use your camera

Take lots of photos throughout the project! As time goes by, I love to go through my old scrapbooks and see all the work that went into the cars. If you take your car to shows, leave the scrapbooks out for all to see. You will be surprised how much conversation will start. Who knows, if you document the project well enough, maybe you will be writing the next hot rod book. The photos will also be valuable if you ever want to sell the car. They should document all of the hard work as well as the quality that went into your vehicle.

Security

Your scrapbook will be invaluable should the car ever get stolen. Yes, you need to consider this. Street rods are prime candidates for theft. I've been to many shows where cars get stolen right off the show grounds. Every time it happens, we stand around and scratch our heads and ask why. The answer is easy — custom cars are easy to retool and sell. Usually, a team of thieves will go to a show and steal multiple cars and bring them back to their shop. With the replacement of a few tags and a new coat of paint, they can register the car as a new build.

If a '37 Ford is stolen, all the thieves need to do is purchase a rusty '37 and transfer those numbers to the stolen car. Then they wait six months so it looks like they worked on it and sell it for $20,000. Do this a dozen times a year and you are making a pretty good living with little work.

Car alarms are not good enough. I highly recommend that you consider something more advanced, like the Lo Jack system. This technology can be purchased for around $800. With this system your car gets registered in a national database. As soon as your car is reported missing, a signal is transmitted from the police radio network and activates a transmitter in your car. The police follow the signal and locate and retrieve the car for you. The system works so well that many thieves take stolen cars to vacant lots and let them sit. They watch from a distance and wait to see if police come to retrieve the car. They do this because they don't want to lure police to their shop, but the good news is you have a decent chance of getting your car back without a damaging high-speed chase.

Storage

Cars need to be driven. A lot of cars sit throughout the winter and this is hard on a car. Winterize your vehicle by putting the car up on jack stands. This keeps the tires from cracking or developing flat spots. Most importantly, start your car once a week. Modern gasoline has a chemical in it that causes it to gel over time. There are chemicals you can add to your tank to prevent this, but nothing is healthier for an engine than for it to run frequently. This keeps all of your gaskets wet and the moving parts lubricated. Avoid condensation in the tank by keeping it full. The less air in the tank the better. Armor All or silicon spray all the rubber gaskets to keep them from sticking to the steel or cracking.

Washing

Most paint damage is caused by the owners. We have been taught all our lives to "wax-on/wax-off" in circles, but this leaves that spider web effect you see in dark-colored paint. The darker the color, the more noticeable they become. In fact, wax is not what you want to use on urethane paint, anyway. All enamels are softer than lacquer. Whenever you use wax, water beads up on the surface of the paint. These little beads act like magnifying glasses, and the sun will hit these beads and burn tiny marks in the surface of the paint. You are better off not to wash your car at all. If your car has been driven on wet roads or has mud caked on, then yes, you will have to wash it. But if a car is simply dusty, you can use a dust mop to pick up any loose dust particles and then use a hand glaze to bring out the luster in the paint. As long as you rub the glaze in straight lines down the length of the car, you will not get those circular spider web scratches in the paint. Dri Wash 'n Guard is another product that is catching on with rodders and it is used in lieu of hand glaze.

Most of all, rodding is about fun. Almost immediately after your car is finished, some Jackassus Maximus will probably come out of the woodwork and tell you all the things that are wrong with your car. The problem with this subclass of the human species is they think they know everything about hot rods, but don't seem to own one. The truth is, these negative people are just jealous that you persevered and they didn't. You will meet a few of these folks. Try to ignore them and enjoy your car!

Chapter 17

How to Inspect a Shop

A high-quality restoration or hot rod shop will often have a lot going on at once. It's important to observe what's going on in a shop before you commit to any big projects or part with a bunch of your hard-earned money.

A FRIEND OF MINE ASKED ME TO TAG ALONG one day to visit a shop he was considering. I kept quiet and just wandered along with him as the owner showed us around the facility. It was impressive in the sense that it was large with 20,000 square feet or more and had at least two dozen cars in all stages of construction. All the cars were organized neatly in bays and there must have been eight employees all working diligently on various tasks. The shop was clean too, which is a real pet peeve of mine.

I know my friend was impressed and was excited to get on the waiting list to have the shop begin work on his car. On the way home, he asked me what I thought and I had to say that I would pass on doing business with this shop. He was surprised, but professionals have different criteria for judging shops

When you look around, are the employees busy? Are they all working on something and active? These are important details in the shop's work ethic. Also, take a look and see if the employees look happy. The employees do most of the work, not the owner. If the guy that starts your car leaves, how easily can others pick up and finish? I like to ask around and see how long each guy has been there.

Notice the clutter around this car. It's obviously a parts car, but the overall lack of cleanliness here is a problem. Also note that the car is being used as a shelf. Try to look for subtle details or hints to the shop's overall attitude.

This shop obviously has plenty of room and is neat and well organized. These are good indicators the shop has its act together. *(Gibbon Fiberglass Reproductions)*

than most customers.

It is very rare to find a shop that performs every task of a project. First, the investment needed to do mechanical, electrical, upholstery, engine, transmission, paint, bodywork, etc., is cost prohibitive, and the chances that you could find stable employees that have mastered each or all of the skills are very slim. Most shops focus on their individual specialization and farm certain "extras" out to other shops. For example, a good paint booth will cost between $30,000 and $100,000. Shops specializing in paint and bodywork usually farm out chrome, engine builds and upholstery to other shops to save time and money. However, the shop that gets the car first is technically responsible for all the work the other shops do, so most professionals have certain things they look for when evaluating other shops.

There were things I liked about the shop we visited. First, cleanliness is crucial. Dirty shops have a tendency to lose things. It's also a pride thing. If you don't have any pride in your shop, why should I expect you to take pride in your work?

I also like to see plenty of shelves near all the cars with bagged and labeled parts neatly stacked in place. On some cars where certain replacement screws can cost hundreds of dollars, so you just can't afford to lose parts. You also have to consider that as time goes by, you won't remember what all the parts look like or where they go. Clearly labeled and neatly stored parts make the entire construction go smoothly. The same goes for the office. People

that have paper piles all over the place also have a tendency to lose things.

Space is also important. When a car is completely disassembled, it can easily take up four times as much space. Shoebox-sized shops just don't seem to work well. About 600 to 800 sq. ft. per car is needed to be effective.

Pay special attention to the employees and how they are working. Hot rod building takes perseverance and diligence. I have found that the two

Some shops insist on organization and neatness. This business neatly stores removed parts on a clean shelving unit.

If possible, hang around and watch some of the work taking place. It can be educational to watch a painter working at his craft, and can also reveal what kind of work habits the shop personnel have.

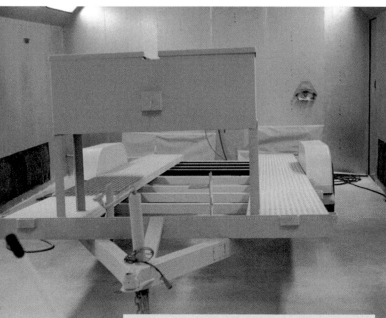

Lighting and cleanliness are key to high-quality work. I like to take a look at the painting area to see if it is up to date and clean.

don't always go together.

Perseverance has a tendency to come easy for employees. As long as they are getting paid, they can persevere through just about anything. It is different for hobbyists, however. It's hard to find free time to work on cars, especially if small children are anywhere in the picture. If a project stalls or gets set aside, it just seems too easy to abandon the project altogether.

Diligence is something completely different.

People seem to care more about things they own, but have a tendency to slack off a bit if it belongs to someone else. Employees may cut corners when the boss isn't looking and that is hard to control for shop owners. I study the employee to see if they are focused on their work or if they are looking away or daydreaming. Do they seem to talk amongst themselves constantly or wander around the shop? I've walked into a shop many times and have seen everybody drinking beer! There is work time and play time. Do they really mix? Would you want someone assembling your steering linkage after a six-pack? Any one of these things would be a deal breaker for me.

There are other things I look for too, like employee-to-car ratio. In this case, there were eight employees and 24 cars. If a complete project takes 1 or 2 years to complete when working full-time, then it's likely your car will sit in the shop 6 years or so if they have a 3:1 car to employee ratio. The only way to reduce that number is to cut corners and all too often that is what shops decide to do. I look for shops with a 1.5 car-to-employee ratio or less, so in our example, it would be better if the shop had 8 employees and only 12 cars. That was the first thing I noticed that I didn't like.

The second was that I noticed the shop had a racing team and I could see the trailer and race car parked out back. Now, there are plenty of shops with race teams that produce good work, but I have had several negative adventures with them. In my experiences, it just seemed that the owners used the shop as a means to support their true passion, which

The type of cars a shop has on hand can offer a clue to what kind of business it is running. Here a worker is fabricating a fender for a Ferrari. Seeing high-dollar cars on the premises can be a good sign that the shop has earned a solid reputation among car owners.

was racing. I feel uncomfortable doing business with anyone who doesn't have all of their attention and resources focused on the work at hand. The attitude I got at several of these shops was "Yeah, yeah, just put it over there and we'll call you later with the estimate." That's not good enough for me and it seemed all of these shops were either overpriced or took too long to complete the work. I no longer do business with anybody that has a shop-supported distraction like racing.

The last tip is perhaps the most obvious, but seems to be overlooked because it takes time: Get a reference or referral. Let someone else be the guinea pig. It is crucial to speak with someone that actually did business with the shop before you and puts their personal recommendation on it. If there is a consistent problem with quality, billing or customer service, then the person before you probably knows about it.

A full-service shop may even offer upholstery services.

Resources

3M
3M Center Building 223-6N-01
St Paul, MN 55144
www.mmm.com

A & M SoffSeal Inc.
104 May Drive
Harrison OH 45030
www.soffseal.com

A.C.E. Sand Blasting Equipment
897 South Washington PMB 232
Holland, MI 49423

Advanced Plating
955 East Trinity Lane
Nashville, TN 37207
www.advancedplating.com

AFCO Hot Rod Products
P.O. Box 548
Booneville, IN 47601
www.hotrodafco.com

Affordable Street Rods
1220 Van Buren
Great Bend, KS 67530
www.affordablestreetrods.com

Air Ride Technologies Inc.
2762 Cathy Drive
Jasper, IN 47546

Alumicraft Street Road Grilles
308 South Fourth St.
Bellwood, PA 16617
www.alumicraft.com

American Autowire
150 Heller Place #17W
Bellmawr, NJ 08031

American Racing Custom Wheels
19067 South Reyes Ave.
Rancho Dominguez, CA 90221
www.americanracing.com

American Stamping
8650 Mid-South Drive
Oilve Branch, MS 38654

Authentic Zombie Hot Rod Wear
4990 Creston Valley Road
PO Box 279 Creston, CA 93432
ww.zombiehotrodwear.com

Auto Chic
P.O. Box 6181
West Caldwell, NJ 07007
www.liquidglass.com

Auto Meter Products
413 West Elm St.
Sycamor, IL 60178
www.autometer.com

Autoweek
1400 Woodbridge Ave.
Detroit, MI 48207
www.autoweek.com

B & M Racing & Performance Products
9142 Independence Ave.
Chatsworth, CA 91311
www.bmracing.com

Backyard Buddy Corp.
140 Dana St.
Warren, OH 44483
www.backyardbuddy.com

Ball's Rod & Kustom
10121 North State Road 13
Syracuse, IN 46567
www.ballsrodandkustom.com

Beugler Stripers
3667 Tracy St.
Los Angeles, CA 90039
www.beugler.com

B F Goodrich Tires
One Parkway South
Greenville, SC 29602
www.bfgoodrichtires.com

Billet Specialties Inc.
340 Shore Drive
Burr Ridge, IL 60521
billetspecialties.com

Bob Drake Reproductions Inc.
1899 NW Hawthorne Ave.
Grants Pass, OR 97526
www.bobdrake.com

Borgeson Universal Co. Inc.
187 Commercial Blvd.
Torrington, CT 06790
www.borgeson.com

Brite Ideas
1420 Shell Flower Drive
Brandon, FL 33571

Buckaroo Communications Inc.
12434 Prescilla Road
Camarillo, CA 93012
wwwsuperrod.com
www.streetrodbuilder.com

Busch Enterprises Inc.
908 Cochran St.
Statesville, NC 28677

California Car Cover Co.
9525 DeSoto Ave.
Chatsworth, CA 91311
www.calcarduster.com

Chevrolet Motor Division
100 Renaissance Center
Detroit, MI 48265
www.chevrolet.com

City Glass & Upholstery
1943 Tacoma Ave. South
Tacoma, WA 98402
www.cityglass.net/Automobiles.html

Classic Enterprises
P.O. Box 1162
Pleasantville, NJ 08232
www.classicenterprises.com

Coker Tire
1317 Chestnut St.
Chattanooga, TN 37402
www.coker.com

Colorado Custom
2421 International
Ft. Collins, CO 80524
www.coloradocustom.com

Crossfire Mfg.
P.O. Box 263
Sharpsville, PA 16150

Custom Rodtronics
22105 Westwind Dr.
Elkhorn, NE 68022

C.W. Moss Ford Parts Inc.
402 West Chapman Ave.
Orange CA 92866
www.cwmoss.com

Dakota Digital
3421 West Hovland Ave.
Sioux Falls, SD 57107
www.dakotadigital.com

Danny's Rod Shop
1853 Old State Rt. 28
Goshen, OH 45122

Debnam's Paint and Body, Inc.
7905 Hwy 64 East
Knightdale, NC 27545

Denver Specialty Center
7801 East Colfax
Denver, CO 80220

Design Engineering Inc.
36960 Detroit Road
Avon, OH 44011

Downs Mfg.
715 North Main St.
Lawton, MI 49065

DuPont Automotive Finishes
312 Center St.
Farmington, MO 63640
www.dupont.com/finishes

Eagle One
5927 Landau Ct.
Carlsbad, CA 92008
www.eagleone.com

Earl's Performance Products
189 West Victoria St.
Long Beach, CA 90805
www.earlsperformance.com

Eaton Detroit Spring Inc.
1555 Michigan
Detoit, MI 48216
www.eatonsprings.com

Edelbrock
2700 California Ave.
Torrance, CA 90503
www.edelbrock.com

Emgee/Clean Tools
10 Plaza Drive
Westmont, IL 60559
www.emgee@mcs.net

Engineered Components Inc.
P.O. Box 841
Vernon, CT 06066

Fatman Fabrications Inc.
8621-C Fairview Road Hwy 218
Charlotte, NC 28227-7619
www.fatmanfab.com

Flaming River Industries Inc.
800 Poertner Drive
Berea, OH 44017
www.flamingriver.com

Ford Racing
14555 Rotunda Drive Suite 131
Dearborn, MI 48120
www.fordracing.com

GM Performance Parts
6200 Grand Pointe Drive
Grand Blanc, MI 48439
www.gmgoodwrench.com

Gibbon Fiberglass Reproductions
132 Industrial Way
Darlington, SC 29532
www.gibbonfiberglass.com

Godman Hi-Performance
5255 Elmore Road
Memphis, TN 38134
www.godmanhiperformance.com

Goldcoast Coating
19 Aviador Unit A
Camarillo, CA 93010

Goldeez Hot Rod Products
400 Easton Drive Suite 1
Bakersfield, CA 93309
www.goldeez.com

Goodyear Tire
1144 East Market St.
Akron, OH 44316
www.goodyear.com

Grooms Engines
611 4th Ave South
Nashville, TN 37210
www.groomsengines.com

Hagan Street Rod Necessities
2179 Joanne Drive #4
Carson City, NV 89701
www.haganstreetrods.com

Haneline Products Co.
P.O. Box 430
Morongo Valley, CA 92256

Haywire Inc.
1415 Prairie View Road
Joplin, MO 64804
www.haywireinc.com

Heidt's Hot Rod Shop
1345 North Old Rand Road
Wauconda, IL 60084

Hercules Motor Car Co.
2502 North 70th St.
Tampa, FL 33619
www.herculesmotorcarcompany.com

Holley Performance Products
1801 Russellville Road
Bowling Green, KY 42102
www.holley.com

Hotrod Hotline
10400 Overland Road #402
Boise, ID 83709
www.hotrodhotline.com

House of Kolor/Valspar
210 Crosby St.
Picayune, MS 39466
www.houseofkolor.com

Howron Industries
1915 Laurelwood Drive
Denton, TX 76201

HPC
550 West 3615 South
Salt Lake City, UT 84115
www.hpcoatings.com

Inland Empire Driveline
4035 East Guasti Road #302
Ontario, CA 91761

Insulshield Technologies
207 Cushing St.
Hingham, MA 02043
www.insulshield.net

Interiors by Shannon
907 Overhill Drive
Alexander City, AL 35010
www.interiorsbyshannon.com

Jake's Pinstriping
8309 Hwy 80 West
Ft. Worth, TX 76116
www.jakespinstriping.com

Jet Hot Coatings Division MCCI
55 East Front St.
Bridgeport, PA 19405
www.jethot1.com

Juliano's Interior Products
321 Talcotteville Road
Vernon, CT 06066
www.julianos.com

Kemps Rod and Restoration, Inc.
636 Industrial Park Drive
Iron Mountain, MI 49801
www.exploringthenorth.com/kemp/rods.html

Kimberly-Clark/Scott DIY Business
300 Chesterfield Center Suite 200
Chesterfield, MO 63017

KWIKLIFT INC.
610 North Walnut
Broken Arrow, OK 74012
www.kwiklift.com

Kwik Poly
P.O. Box 12330
O'Fallon, MO 63366

Lokar Inc.
10924 Murdock Drive
Knoxville, TN 37932

Made For You Products
P.O. Box 720700
Pinon Hills, CA 92372
www.made4uproducts.com

McGard Inc.
3875 California Road
Orchard Park, NY 14127
www.mcgard.com

Meguiar's Inc.
17991 Mitchell St.
Irvine, CA 92614
www.meguiars.com

Miller Electric
1635 West Spencer St.
Appleton, WI 54914

Mr. Gasket Co.
10601 Memphis Ave. #12
Cleveland, OH 44144
www.mrgasket.com

Mullins Steering Gears
2876 Sweetwater Ave. #2
Lake Havasu City, AZ 86406
www.mullinssteeringgears.com

Old Chicago Street Rods
16169 SE 106
Clackamas, OR 97015

Outlaw Performance Inc.
P.O. Box 550 Rt. 380 Nelson
Avonmore, PA 15618
www.outlawrods.com

Parr Automotive
4933 NW 10th St.
Oklahoma City, OK 73127
www.parrautomotive.com

P-Ayr Products
719 Delaware St.
Leavenworth, KS 66048
www.payr.com

Pete & Jakes Hot Rod Parts
401 Legend Lane
Peculiar, MO 64078
www.peteandjakes.com

Powermaster
2401 Dutch Valley Road
Knoxville, TN 37918
www.powermastermotorsports.com

PPG Industries Inc.
19699 Progress Drive
Strongsville, OH 44136
www.ppg.com

Pro-Blend Motorsports
830 Manly St.
Winston Salem, NC 27101

RB's Obsolete Auto
7711 Lake Ballinger Way
Edmonds, WA 98026
www.rbsobsolete.com

Richmond Gear
1208 Old Norris Road
Liberty, SC 29657

Rocky Hinge Co.
1720 Wilson Ave.
Girard, OH 44420

Rod Doors
PO Box 2160
Chico, CA 95927
www.roddoors.com

Ron Francis Wire Works
167 Keystone Road
Chester, PA 19013
www.wire-works.com

Sanderson Street Rod Headers
517 Railroad Ave.
San Francisco, CA 94080
www.sandersonheaders.com

Sharp Enterprises
1005 Cole St.
Laclede, MO 64651

Showtime Automobile Accessories
899 North Market St.
Selinsgrove, PA 17870

Sneed Robinson & Gerber Inc.
6645 Stage Road
Bartlett, TN 38134
www.sneedcompanies.com

Southern Rods & Parts Inc.
2125 Airport Road
Greer, SC 29650
www.southernrods.com

Springfield Street Rod
219 Buxton
Springfield, OH 45505
www.springfieldstreetrods.com

Stewart Warner Instruments
200 Howard Ave. Bldg. 250
Des Plaines, IL 60018
www.stewartwarner.com

Stinger by Axe Equipment
Hwy 177 North/P.O. Box 296
Council Grove, KS 66846
www.stingerlifts.com

Street Rods by Michael
120 Deery St
Shelbyville, TN 37160-4024
(931) 680-0010

Street Rod Digital
14241 NE Woodinville-Duvall Road #101
Woodinville, WA 98072
www.streetroddigital.com

Street & Performance Inc.
Rt 5 #1 Hot Rod Lane
Mena, AR 71953
www.hotrodlane.cc

Street Rodder Magazine
2400 East Katella St.
Anaheim, CA 92806
www.streetrodderweb.com

TD Performance
16410 Manning Way
Cerritos, CA 90703
www.tdperformance.com

Tea's Design
2038 15th St. NW
Rochester, MN 55901
www.teasdesign.com

The Eastwood Company
580 Lancaster Ave. P.O. Box 296
Malvern, PA 19355
www.eastwoodcompany.com

The Lincoln Electric Co.
22801 St. Clair Ave.
Cleveland, OH 44117
www.lincolnelectric.com

The Wheel Tough Co.
P.O. Box 10073
Terre Haute, IN 47801
www.wheeltough.com

Total Cost Involved Engineering Inc.
1416 West Brooks St.
Ontario, CA 91762

Total Performance Inc.
400 South Orchard St Rt. 5
Wallingford, CT 06492
www.tperformance.com

TPI Performance Transmissions
231 S. Lindberg
Griffith, IN 46319
www.tpiperformace.com

Ultra Tek
82 Cannas Ct.
Cheektowaga, NY 14227

VDO Performance Instruments
188 Brooke Road
Winchester, VA 22603
vdona.com

Valley Auto Accessories
1554 E. 1333rd Lane
Flower, IL 62338

Village Buffing
902 East 22 St.
Kannapolis, NC 28083

Vintage Air Inc.
10305 IH 35 North
San Antonio, TX 78209
www.vintageair.com

Visibolts
7131 Hickory Lane
Waunakee, WI 53597
www.visibolts.com

Walker Radiator Works
694 Marshall Ave.
Memphis, TN 38103
www.hotrodsworldwide.com/catalogs/walker.htm

Warren Motorsports
7065 West Ann Road #130-207
Las Vegas, NV 89130
www.warren-motorsports.com

Watson's Street Works Rod & Custom
P.O. Box 270
Bozrah, CT 06334
www.watsons-streetworks.com

Weld Wheel Industries Inc.
933 Mulberry St.
Kansas City, MO 64101
weldracing.com

Wescott's Auto Restyling
19701 SE Hwy. 212
Boring, OR 97009
www.wescottsauto.com

William's Welding
14770 Cooks Mills Road
Humboldt, IL 61931

Yearwood Speed & Custom
6830 Gateway East
El Paso, TX 79915
www.yearwood.com

Yogi's Inc.
PO Box 68
Calamus, IA 52729
www.yogisinc.com

Zoops Products Inc.
931 East Lincoln St.
Banning, CA 92220
www.zoops.com